Alcoholic Women in Treatment

Alcoholic Women in Treatment

Eileen M. Corrigan
GRADUATE SCHOOL OF SOCIAL WORK
RUTGERS—THE STATE UNIVERSITY

New York / Oxford
OXFORD UNIVERSITY PRESS
1980

Copyright © 1980 by Oxford University Press, Inc.

Library of Congress Cataloging in Publication Data

Corrigan, Eileen M
   Alcoholic women in treatment.

  Bibliography: p.
  Includes index.
  1. Alcohol and women—Case studies. 2. Temperance—
Case studies. I. Title. [DNLM: 1. Alcoholism—Therapy.
2. Women. WM274.3 C825a]
HV5137.C69   362.2′92′0926   79-17895
ISBN 0-19-502653-5

Printed in the United States of America

To the many women who participated in this study

Preface

In 1978, at a national meeting convened by the National Institute on Alcohol Abuse and Alcoholism (NIAAA) and attended primarily by women researchers, a number of recommendations were forthcoming for future studies of problem drinking. Responding to prepared papers, research needs in five areas were identified: prevention and education; epidemiology; biological and psychosocial consequences; risk factors; and clinical research.

Although all types of research design were encouraged, the longitudinal design was endorsed most frequently. For example, in the area of epidemiology a longitudinal study of women who are known to be heavy drinkers and normal drinkers would include regular sampling, with sub-group analysis. In recognition of the heterogeneity of alcoholic women, speakers at the meeting emphasized again and again the need to gather data on sub-groups of women alcoholics, that is, women of all social classes, minority women, women of different age groups, and so on. Other needs, general and specific, were also defined: a national research center, interdisciplinary in nature, to study the biological and psychosocial aspects of alcohol abuse by women; research on women in a "model" treatment center that would be innovative in its treatment; and research on the results of various treatment modalities, including exclusively women's groups in contrast to mixed gender groups.

The present study, longitudinal in design, began in 1974 with 150 women chosen from a number of treatment settings. The independent variables used in the analysis, Table 2-3, include many of the focal points of concern defined at the 1978 meeting of the NIAAA. This study assumes that the professional work of researchers in all areas of alcohol abuse is a necessary prerequisite if any progress against alcoholism is to occur. It also assumes that another prerequisite must be present if those who suffer from alcohol abuse are to be truly helped: a profound change in society's perceptions of alcoholism.

Most people continue to have an extremely poor understanding of alcohol use. The high potential of alcohol for *inducing dependency* is either not known or ignored. When such a dependency does result, it is still largely viewed as shameful, or wrongly attributed to other causes. Those persons who are nearest to a woman dependent on alcohol frequently fumble in attempts to help her. And, in turning to professional helpers, the families and friends of alcoholic women often do not gain the understanding they seek. Because ignorance about alcoholism is almost universal, even professional help often fails to recognize and treat alcoholism. At the heart of this ignorance is a lack of understanding of the dependence that has developed. This may have the consequence of reinforcing a woman's belief that her pattern of drinking is solely within her control.

This book is about those women—some 150 of them—who have eventually come to acknowledge that their drinking is no longer something they can ignore and about the many who journey back to health.

North Hudson, N.Y. E. M. C.
July 1979

Acknowledgments

It is a most happy time to be able to sit quietly and look back upon several years of work. To acknowledge one's debt is an honorable tradition for an author. In this instance such a debt is easy to disclose. To my friend Ana O. Dumois who consistently supported my efforts. To Joan Gebhardt who shared Ana's optimism and was an aid in innumerable ways, in addition to typing endless drafts of the manuscript. To my mother who sat quietly—a difficult task—while I pondered. To Sandra Anderson who, first as a doctoral candidate and then as a colleague, aided immeasurably in analyzing and writing first drafts of a number of sections. To Ruth Bournazian who offered her wisdom to the analysis and supervised the follow-up. To Alice Helrich who faithfully and carefully assisted in the early, difficult years of translating a study proposal into a reality. To my friends Lucille J. Grow, Elaine Norman, and Bob Jones who read the many drafts. Dr. Norman also served as a consultant at various stages of the data analysis and enthusiastically and consistently supported this work. To Nancy Palmer who helped me to be in touch with so many women's groups. To Geraldine Delaney and Le Clair Bissell who helped me to reach many people. To the more than twenty interviewers who carefully interviewed and assisted so much in locating the women after one year. To the many agencies, their directors, and staff who facilitated the study. To Harriet Fink, programmer, who spent so many hours translating our requests into meaningful computer output. To Jane Li, statistician, formerly of Rutgers University, who willingly gave her unique specialized knowledge. To John Grundy of Columbia University, School of Social Work, whose wizardry as computer specialist and statistician eased the way through the extensive material on treatment outcome. To Al Pawlowski of the National Institute on Alcohol Abuse and Alcoholism whose steady support is appreciated. To Rutgers University, The Graduate School of Social Work, and its Dean Harold Demone who offered the environment needed to carry out such work. To the editor, Jeffrey House, Ellen B. Fuchs, managing editor, and the other able staff of Oxford University Press who from the beginning have helped me move easily to bring this study's results to a wide audience. To Bill Mudie for his most able editorial assistance and Allan Pierce for his warm interest. Finally, to the women who participated in this study, their sisters, and their husbands who also believed in us and in the message we brought: that only by talking with them would we better understand alcoholism in women.

This investigation was supported by Public Health Research Grant No. AA380 from The Alcohol, Drug and Mental Health Administration, National Institute on Alcohol Abuse and Alcoholism. A small grant from The Research Council of Rutgers University and a faculty leave program at Rutgers University in 1977–1978 gave time for the analysis and writing to be completed.

Contents

1
Introduction, 3

Magnitude of problem drinking in women, 5
Life situations and the onset of problem drinking in women, 7
Sexual adjustment, 7
Troubles resulting from drinking, 8
Outcome of treatment, 9

2
The Study Design: Methodology and Analysis Plan, 11

Methodology, 11
Analysis plan, 15

3
Patterns of Drinking, 30

Summary of findings, 30
Onset of drinking and problem drinking, 33

Telescoped drinking, 34
Pressures for drinking, 36
Alcohol consumption, 38
Binge drinkers, 43
Type of alcoholic beverage, 44
Setting and situation of drinking, 44
Drinking among friends and neighbors, 48
Secrecy in drinking, 48
Social-escapist reasons for drinking, 50
Drinking with other drug use, 51
Maintenance of drinking, 54
Summary and conclusions, 55

4
Consequences of Drinking, 60

Summary of findings, 60
Stigma reinforcement, 63
High for more than one day, 65
Perceived social rejection for problem drinking, 66
Social life, 67
Sexual behavior of alcoholic women, 68
Problems as defined by the women, 71
Troubles resulting from drinking, 72
Emotional health, 75
Interference arising from drinking: Family, social, job, and health areas, 78
Correlations between self-ratings of family, social, job, and health problems, 80
Background variables and interference, 81
Conclusions, 83

5
Marriages, Children, and Husbands, 86

Summary of findings, 86
Marriage, 88
Children, 92
Husband interviews, 97
Conclusions, 104

6
The Family in the Etiology of Alcoholism, 107

Summary of findings, 107
Siblings, 111
Sisters—a comparison group, 112
The sisters view each other, 122
Etiology of alcoholism, 124
Conclusions, 128

7
Outcome of Treatment, 131

Summary of findings, 131
The treatment settings, 133
The agency, 137
Outcome of treatment: Effects on drinking, 138
Quantity of alcohol consumed, 139
Background variables and drinking outcome, 139
Emotional health and drinking outcome, 141
Employment and drinking outcome, 144
Prior treatment and drinking outcome, 145
Maintenance dosage of alcohol, 146
Drinking outcome, emotional health score, and treatment, 147

Drinking outcomes, 150
Conclusions, 152

8
Conclusions and Summary: Implications for Intervention, Treatment, and Research, 155

The onset and etiology of problem drinking for women, 157
Effects on self and others, 163
Description of the course of treatment and outcome, 165
Conclusions, 166

Appendix A. Data Base, 169

Appendix B. Statistical Procedures, 177

Bibliography, 181

Index, 187

Alcoholic Women in Treatment

1
Introduction

Research on women and alcohol remains one of the most neglected areas of research in the field of alcohol studies.[1] Conflicting data and beliefs abound on women problem drinkers. But from these beliefs and data, scattered and deficient as they are, certain conclusions are expressed frequently: Women usually turn to drinking because of a specific life situation. Women most often follow a pattern of drinking alone. Women drinkers prove more harmful to themselves and others in their drinking than do men. And women in treatment show poorer results than men.

Because drinking, especially heavy drinking, is generally held to be less acceptable for women than for men, women are said to feel more stigma and shame because of society's nonacceptance of the intoxicated woman. Women are thought to differ from men because they are more likely to be lone, secretive drinkers (Lisansky, 1957; Blane, 1968). In a study of drinking practices, women who drink heavily were reported more likely to be "escapist drinkers" as compared with male "social" drinkers (Knupfer, 1963).

Lisansky (1958) gives cogent reasons to reject the belief that the woman problem drinker is more sick than the male problem drinker; she also points to the more punitive social consequences women must endure as a result of their alcoholism. J. E. deLint (1964) notes that female alcoholics are more frequently found to be deprived of one or more parents at an early age than are male alcoholics. Thus, "they can be expected to respond least favorably to treatment." Here deLint assumes that, regardless of other factors, the loss of a parent at an early age has a similar effect on a child: an almost irreversible emotional deprivation that extends into adult life. Further, deLint assumes that the female problem drinker is at greater disadvantage than the male problem drinker. Such complex assumptions are, of course, unproven.

The effect of having a mother who is a problem drinker is thought to be more "devastating" on children than is the effect of a father who is a problem drinker. Also, a husband is reported to be less likely to remain in a marriage with an alcoholic spouse than is a wife (Kent, 1967). The wife tends to make a greater effort to maintain a marriage in which the husband is a problem drinker. Few studies either support or rebut these specific conclusions.

Although many investigators have written descriptive studies about women as problem drinkers, Lisansky's work in the mid-1950s (1957, 1958) seems to be the latest analytical study of note. More recent writings by Curlee (1967, 1968, 1969, 1970, 1971) give attention to the woman problem drinker and explore the validity of clinical theory as it relates to women alcoholics. Subsequently, Wilsnack (1973) explored sex role identification and Beckman (1978) the self-esteem of alcoholic women.

In her work, Lisansky (1957) reported that women begin their drinking at a later date than men and appear for treatment after fewer years of problem drinking. Horn and Wanberg (1971) supported this conclusion in finding that although women start drinking later than men, they come to the hospital at an earlier state in the development of their alcoholism than men do. A contradictory conclusion was reached—in another setting—by Chafetz et al. (1970). They reported a greater average duration of excessive drinking for women before they come for treatment and speculated that women may be more reluctant than men to seek therapy early.

On the other hand, researchers agree that a belief in the close relationship between alcohol and sexual promiscuity of women drinkers is unfounded. It is one of the myths generated by limited knowledge of women and their problems as alcoholics. Most writers also concede that information about marital and familial relationships of women problem drinkers is grievously lacking. Lisansky (1957) early pointed to the plenitude of studies of the wives of problem drinkers and to the nonexistence of studies of the husbands of problem drinkers. This disproportionate lack of information persists.

Yet Curlee (1967) correctly observes that alcoholism among women is being brought more and more to the level of public awareness: More women are now known to be alcoholic than in previous years. Lisansky (1958) noted that "in the vast literature on alcoholism there are only two reports on alcoholic women which go beyond statistical summary or mere conjecture." More than ten years after this statement of Lisansky, Curlee (1967) was to say that "studies on alcoholism tend either to ignore women entirely or simply to assume that alcoholism is the same, regardless of the sex of the sufferer."

In recent decades, the majority of the studies about problem drinkers omit women, usually without comment. Perhaps their authors deem women to represent too small a proportion of problem drinkers in a particular treatment setting to justify their inclusion. Perhaps they consider that this lack of data will limit their scope of generalization. Perhaps they also feel that the methodological problems of accumulating a sufficiently large sample of women are too complex and time consuming—an undertaking that does not promise to reveal significant differences in results over all-male studies. On the other hand, perhaps the researchers to date have had, for unexamined and unjustified reasons, less interest in females as problem drinkers.

Let us review here, then, the research on women problem drinkers to identify those aspects that have already received adequate attention and to pinpoint those areas most likely in need of early study so that basic and current descriptive information may be obtained about women as problem drinkers.

Magnitude of problem drinking in women

The extent of problem drinking among women is not known with certainty. Although prevalence figures continue to be debated, the evidence points increasingly to a lower national ratio, possibly as low as 4 : 1 rather than the 5 : 1 male-female ratio reported more than a quarter of a century ago by Keller and Efron (1955). Such a drop was expected; for, at the time of the Keller and Efron study, female drinkers were said to be increasing more than twice as fast as male drinkers. In this early analysis, however, it was not possible to determine whether or not problem drinking among women was marked by distinctive trends; nor was it possible to account for the large differences in the changes between rates of male and female alcoholism within certain states. These data, which are derived from cirrhosis mortality statistics, are vulnerable, of course, to all the errors inherent in regional variations in reporting the cause of deaths. In addition, such statistics have been challenged increasingly in principle as a basis for estimating the prevalence of alcoholism.[2]

In a growth study in Oakland, California, M. C. Jones (1971) found fewer sex differences in the data on alcoholics than were reported in most studies and attributed this similarity to the respondents being predominantly urban, middle class, and middle aged. In Cahalan's (1970) data from a national sample, the ratio is approximately 3 : 1 males to females reporting either symptomatic drinking or psychological dependence on alcohol.

When the male-female ratio is based on an examination of data on women who come to the attention of a particular community resource, these ratios vary even more widely. Keller and Efron (1955) report 11 : 1 males to females in police custody; 6 : 1 in hospitals; 4 : 1 in social agencies; and 3 : 1 with private physicians. Gerard and Sanger (1966) find a ratio of 6 : 1 males to females in state-supported alcoholism clinics, and we (Corrigan, 1974a) compute a ratio of closer to 4 : 1 in a New York City referral service for problem drinkers.

Cahn (1970) compares male and female alcoholics both in total admissions and in first admissions to state and county mental hospitals. In 1963, there was a ratio of 5.5 : 1 male to female admissions. To determine if there was any shift in the male-female ratio over a recent five- to six-year period, these admissions data were updated. By 1969 (United States Department of Health, Education, and Welfare, 1968), the ratio was 4.2 : 1, demonstrating the expected change in total admissions. First admissions in 1963 showed a ratio of 4.09 : 1, and by 1968 (United States Department of Health, Education, and Welfare, 1969), male to female admissions had narrowed to 3.4 : 1.

All the available information points, then, to a progressively lower estimated ratio of males to females as problem drinkers in both the general population and among those who appear for treatment. At a minimum, women problem drinkers comprise one million of the estimated problem drinkers, if five million is accepted as a minimal estimate of the number of problem drinkers in this country. Bell (1971) notes that a similar ratio of alcoholism between men and women would be a good social indicator of the changed status of women: "One measurement of total sexual equality's having been reached will be when there are no differences in alcoholic rates among men and women." Such a view of alcoholism as an indicator of equality may well be challenged.

Life situations and the onset of problem drinking in women

Wall (1937) is apparently the first to have observed that excessive drinking in women is associated with a definite life situation. This view is subsequently repeated by other writers on the subject. Later, Lolli (1953) stated that precipitating factors are more important in women than men, pointing to biological phenomena with accompanying depression as precipitating uncontrolled drinking. Still later, and in much the same vein, Curlee (1969) stated "alcoholism in women is more often associated with a particular life situation or problem, than is the case with male alcoholics." In 1970, Sclare also reported his findings about women alcoholics on the basis of specific situations precipitating problem drinking.

Although the variety of specific life situations cited by these authors is almost exhaustive of the possible problems that a woman can encounter, nowhere does this variety provide any understanding of the choice of heavy drinking. Curlee (1969), in fact, points to a swift onset of problem drinking after a loss. Lisansky (1957) while disputing a cause-effect relationship between heavy drinking and physiology supports the idea that pressures in the environment may precipitate alcoholism in women more than it does in men.

Sexual adjustment

As might be expected, the area of sexual behavior of female problem drinkers has also received attention. Levine (1955) suggests that the characteristic sexual problem of women problem drinkers in his study was frigidity, sometimes associated with promiscuity, but more frequently associated with inhibition and lack of interest. Earlier, Curran (1937) also noted the frequency of frigidity among his subjects. In their study of 69 women, all of whom were from middle to upper socioeconomic backgrounds Wood and Duffy (1966) reported that promiscuity was never a problem for the women. Myerson (1959), however, in studying a group of women prisoners described as alcoholic, called attention to their "wild bouts of promiscuity." These data generally tend to support Lisansky's (1958) contention that sexual promiscuity is more likely to be associated with a particular subgroup of women problem drinkers.

Troubles resulting from drinking

In measuring troubles that usually arise from drinking, investigators tend to weigh heavily those external activities that bring individuals into conflict with employers or the police. There is some evidence that women, while on the job, may hide their problem drinking more than men; also, the police may more often ignore the recalcitrant women. As a result, women drinkers generally have been shown to have fewer troubles than men as a result of their drinking.

We conducted a study (Corrigan, 1974a) of an information and referral service for problem drinkers and found that one in five of the women drinkers who themselves called for help stated they had not experienced any of the six troubles reviewed.[3] Surrogates who called for help about women problem drinkers reported one in twenty as having one of these troubles. In this same study while the women were less likely than men to have such troubles the women with such troubles most frequently reported health or spouse troubles. In contrast, men more often said they had troubles on their jobs. Only one of 69 women studied had as many as five or six of these troubles, whereas 28 of 237 men had this many troubles. These findings are not dissimilar to those of Edwards and associates (1972). Using an extensive list of 25 troubles, they found that no women reported the presence of 10 items. Rather than pursuing the reasons for women experiencing fewer troubles, this British team asks instead why women drink less since those women who do consume as much as men "experience no significant difference in trouble."

Outcome of treatment

Data on the outcome of treatment by gender is especially scant (Blane and Hill, 1967). On the basis of studying 50 males and 50 females, Pemberton (1967) states the prognosis is significantly poorer for females and a disturbed marital relationship is especially related to poor outcome for female problem drinkers. It was hypothesized that females find it more difficult to establish a satisfying role for themselves within their families because of an openly critical husband, a more severely disturbing illness, or a failure to adapt to the loss of a husband.

In contrast, Gerard and Sanger (1966) report no relationship between gender and the outcome of treatment: "The same proportion of men as of women became abstinent or controlled drinkers although there were some differences within the female patient population." Among women, "housewives showed the greatest improvement. . . . When they were compared with women patients who were otherwise employed, the former were found to have improved roughly twice as often as the latter." This finding is supported by our study of problem drinkers (Corrigan, 1974a) seen at a wide variety of treatment resources in New York City. We found no difference by gender between the proportion of women and men who were still in treatment 45 days after they first communicated with an information service for a referral.

Curlee (1971) has commented on differences in attitudes toward an alcoholism treatment program. She reports significant differences among the personal characteristics and attitudes of both men and women patients, as well as significant differences between the groups.

It is clear that we lack certain basic descriptive data about women who are problem drinkers in contrast to men who are problem drinkers. What appears critical to determine is: (1) the onset and course of progressive drinking for women; (2) the consequences of problem drinking for themselves and for others; and (3) an understanding of the treatment outcomes for women. These are the goals of the research study reported on the following pages.

Innumerable questions are raised or implied in this review of the "state of knowledge" about women alcoholics. To begin to answer these questions and to provide basic descriptive data about alcoholic women, we conducted a study of women entering treatment. In chapter two, we discuss the methodology and analysis plan for the study; in chapter three, the patterns of drinking that women establish; and in chapter four, the varied consequences women suffer from their drinking. In chapter five, we summarize our interviews with the husbands of the women alcoholics studied; and the effects on the children, who were not interviewed. In chapter six, we explore aspects of family histories in the context of theories of alcoholism. In this same chapter, we report on interviews with non-alcoholic sisters. Next, in chapter seven, we present the treatment outcomes for the women under study one year later. Finally, in our concluding chapter, we not only summarize the earlier chapters but also spell out in some detail the implications of this study for alcoholic women, especially those relating to treatment and early intervention.

Notes

1. Much of this review of the literature was prepared for the research proposal that was submitted to the National Institute for Alcohol Abuse and Alcoholism for funding in 1972. It subsequently was revised and appeared as an article in *Addictive Diseases* (Corrigan, 1974b). Since this earlier review, research on women alcoholics has not expanded substantially. Later references are cited throughout subsequent chapters.
2. Brenner, B., 1959. "Estimating The Prevalence of Alcoholism: Towards a Modification of The Jellinek Formula." *Quarterly Journal of Studies on Alcohol,* 20:255–260. Jellinek, E. M., 1959. "Estimating The Prevalence of Alcoholism: Modified Values in The Jellinek Formula and An Alternative Approach." *Quarterly Journal of Studies on Alcohol,* 20:261–269. Wallgren, H. and Barry, H. III 1970. "Actions of Alcohol," Vol. 2 *Chronic and Clinical Aspects,* Elsevier, Amsterdam. Cleary, P. D., 1978. "Some Considerations in Using Cirrhosis Mortality Rates as Indicators of The Prevalence of Alcoholism." *Journal of Studies on Alcohol,* 39:1639–1642.
3. Work, spouse, money, police, health, hospitalization.

2
The Study Design: Methodology and Analysis Plan

Methodology
SCOPE OF THE STUDY

This is a study of alcoholic women as well as their sisters and their husbands—and the agencies they turn to for treatment. It is basically a descriptive, longitudinal study of women who were interviewed for the first time as research subjects when they entered hospitals, clinics, and Alcoholics Anonymous (AA) groups for treatment of alcoholism. The initial interviews of 150 women began at the hospitals and clinics in March 1974 and were completed by the spring of 1975; follow-up interviews, most of which took place in the women's homes, began in February 1975 and were completed for 116 women by June 1976. An average of 13 months elapsed between the first and second interviews.

Interviews also took place with 33 non-alcoholic sisters and with 20 husbands. Agency staff who had primary treatment responsibility completed questionnaires at the beginning and ending of treatment, or one year after the women entered treatment, whichever came first.

An additional smaller group of homeless alcoholic women (31) were interviewed as they entered a municipally supported shelter for the homeless between October 1974 and February 1975. Efforts to reach the homeless women one year later were relatively unsuccessful; and although extensive tracing procedures were utilized, it was decided that funding resources and time could be allocated more productively to the larger study group. A report on the homeless women will be published separately.

SAMPLE SELECTION

Women entering treatment. Critical to the sample selection was the decision to interview women just as they *entered* treatment for alcoholism. Obviously, it would have been considerably simpler to select women who are currently in treatment. This latter approach was discarded since it would interfere with studying the natural course of treatment. Clearly, a sample of women currently in treatment would lose the opportunity to interview many women who attend only a few sessions and then do not continue. Instead, we took *all* consecutive admissions, beginning with a specified date agreed upon by each of the 14 settings that participated in the study. We usually sought 10 outpatients and 5 inpatients from each type of setting. Somewhat different procedures needed to be developed for the women seen from the AA groups. We sought recent members and asked to interview all women who affiliated in the past *three* months. With the exception of the AA women, almost all the research interviews took place on the women's first outpatient visit, and usually within one week of their admission as inpatients.

Agency selected by type of service and auspices. Patients from a number of inpatient facilities, outpatient services, and AA groups were the source of the study group. A wide range of treatment settings were purposely sought for the selection of the alcoholic women to enable us to generalize the study results more readily to "women in treatment." In all, 127 women were selected from 14 treatment settings located in both urban and suburban communities. An additional 23 women were selected from four AA groups, one in the metropolitan region and three in nearby suburbs. The final choice of the agencies (hospitals, clinics, and so on) for the study group was made after an exhaustive review of all possible treatment settings available to women alcoholics in the two locales.

An additional criterion was the volume of female patients. Current data on admissions by gender were obtained for the prior year (1972) from each of the settings in the two study locales. Based on the data collected, an average of eight or more women as outpatients and three or more women as inpatients admitted monthly was the cutoff figure for agency eligibility. Finally, the agencies were stratified by their inpatient and outpatient services. The inpatient-outpatient stratification was an effort to reach women who are possibly at different stages of their alcoholism and women who may have differing treatment needs.

At no point was it necessary to use random numbers to carry out the agency selection. Either the agency was eliminated because the volume was too small, or the setting was already selected because it provided both outpatient and inpatient services.

Sampling strategy. A comment is in order about the sampling methods applied in this study. Our possible pool included all inpatient and outpatient alcoholic women entering treatment during the recruitment phase of the study. The sampling procedures described are based on those used in a study by Gerard and Sanger (1966) who interviewed consecutive new admissions of patients at state-supported outpatient alcoholism clinics; they subsequently compared them to all other patients and reported the patients not varying significantly on such critical variables as age, marital status, education, occupation, and duration of alcohol problems.

Urban-suburban women. It was believed that the life styles, including the roles and values of women, would vary considerably with the residential areas in which they lived. For this reason, a decision was made to study women from both urban and suburban areas in the Northeast. A large metropolitan city of one eastern state was the locale for the urban women, and a second adjacent northeastern state was the area from which the suburban women were chosen.

Professional women. As part of this same study group, it was believed that a substantial group of professional women should be interviewed. Because these women are probably exposed earlier than other women are to rapid changes in roles, it was thought this might prove to be related to problem drinking. Initially, no special effort was made to select professional women for the study; rather there was a monitoring of the sample by professional status. When it became apparent that two particular suburban private settings were the major source of professional women, we returned to these settings and also to AA groups to increase the proportion of professional women to be included in the study. Some 40 professional women in all, from both the urban and suburban locales, became part of the study group of 150 women. Further details on this group can be found in the analysis plan for the study.

Non-alcoholic sisters. The inclusion of a comparison group of non-alcoholic sisters was to serve several purposes. We hoped it would provide some clues to etiology of the drinking problems in the group of alcoholic women. The primary purpose, however, was to guard against drawing false conclusions about the alcoholic subjects.

To be included in the study, however, it was not necessary for an alcoholic woman to have a non-alcoholic sister, and even if she had one she could withhold permission for an interview with her. Within these limits, 33 usable sister interviews were eventually obtained. Data, however, were collected from each alcoholic subject about her own life experiences as she compared them with those of the non-alcoholic sister (86 in all) closest to her in age.

Husbands. Interviews with husbands were planned primarily to determine if congruence existed between the spouses in a number of areas. Also, data on the husbands of alcoholic women were sorely lacking at the time this study was designed. It was not necessary for the women to be currently married to become a study subject; 47 of the 150 women were living with their husbands at the time of the interview, and 20 of these husbands were interviewed.

Additional details on the interviewing experience, content of the six schedules used in the study, the interviewers, and the response to the research are included in Appendix A. There the sample loss of study women is described with data provided on the differences between those seen and those not seen at the follow-up interview. The coding procedures that were followed are also included in Appendix A.

Analysis plan

This section is intended for those readers who wish to know how such variables as the socioeconomic status and the usual quantities of alcohol the women drink were conceptualized and measured. In all, ten variables are described and their relationship to each other is discussed in some detail so that others may be able to either replicate the measures used, or deviate with knowledge.

These variables are used throughout the following chapters since all of the areas studied were examined against these background variables, and they form the heart of the plan for describing the development and progression of alcoholism in women. Some readers may wish to move to the next chapter and then come back to obtain details of such demographic variables as place of residence, professional employment, race, age, marriage, religion, and agency status.

CONCEPTUALIZATION OF BACKGROUND VARIABLES

The first eight variables described below were viewed as critical, independent demographic characteristics against which all the major descriptive dependent variables would be examined. Two additional variables, not clearly demographic, were also used in the analysis. The conceptualization of each variable will be discussed.

Locale: Urban or suburban place of residence. This particular category was the basis for designating the geographic areas from which the women were selected (see previous section on methodology). Each suburban address was subsequently reviewed for its urban-suburban status; although we originally planned to have 75 women in each group, there was a need to reclassify 13 of the suburban women into the urban category; using 1970 census data it was found they lived in areas classified as urban by the state in which they resided.

Professional employment. This variable also played a major role in selecting the women for the study. Interest in the changing role of women was thought likely to be more in evidence for the women in the professions, and thus we oversampled this group. Forty professional women were ultimately part of the final study group; they were primarily teachers, mostly secondary and grade school, nurses, social workers, and some women in middle-level managerial positions. Although several women were in the arts, none of the higher-status professions, such as those in university teaching, medicine, dentistry, or the law, were represented in this particular study group.

Marital and outside employment status. The combination of marital status and employment outside the home was viewed as a key variable in several of the early analyses of data about working women. Previous research, especially relating to mental health (Huber, 1973), has shown this classification to be meaningful. This variable consists of four categories: currently married and employed, currently married and not employed; not currently or ever married and employed, not currently or ever married and not employed.

Socioeconomic status (SES). This variable was developed for this study since all previous indexes of socioeconomic status for women have been based on the male as the primary wage earner (Acker, 1973). It is a thorny concept for women, especially when some may still be financially dependent. Occupation has been reported to correlate highly with all socioeconomic indicators and is the basis for the Hollingshead Index of Social Position (ISP), along with income (Hollingshead, 1957). Occupation alone is obviously a poor indicator of a woman's social status since many do not work. And to use a husband's income and occupation is also a poor classification conceptually. Also many of the women would not be married. The scheme in Table 2–1 is seen as an improvement over others used for women, but does not completely resolve some of the issues just raised (Jenkins and Norman, 1972).

Two variables formed the basis for this index: the respondent's education and her income (both its source and amount). No weighting was done for any combination from these two categories since all items were considered of equal importance. It was possible for the women to obtain scores between 2 and 10. Thus women with a score of 2 were always those who had less than a high school education and received public assistance or had no income. Those having a score of ten would have to be college graduates (or have higher education) and an income of $20,000 or more yearly. Scores of 3 through 7 could be any combination of education and of source and amount of in-

The Study Design: Methodology and Analysis Plan

TABLE 2-1 *Socioeconomic Index: Education, Source of Income, and Amount of Family Income*

NO. SCORE	EDUCATION	NO. SCORE	SOURCE OF INCOME & AMOUNT OF FAMILY INCOME
14 (1)	Less than high school	32 (1)	Public assistance or no income
39 (2)	Some high school	31 (2)	All other[a]
35 (3)	High school graduate	31 (3)	Employment[b]–less than $9,999
32 (4)	Some college	39 (4)	Employment–($10,000–$19,999)
30 (5)	College graduate or higher	17 (5)	Employment–($20,000 or more)
150		150	

[a] "All other" means the main source of income is from the family (an employed child as distinct from oneself or employed spouse), unemployment insurance, workmen's compensation, social security or other pension, savings, or other source whenever no answer was provided about family income.
[b] "Employment" refers either to the woman's employment, to her spouse's, or to the employment of both.

come. "Some high school" (score 2) and employment with an income of between $10,000 and $19,999 (score 4) would give a total score of 6. Also, a high school graduate whose source of income was employment with an income of less than $9,999 could achieve a similar score, Table 2-2.

Cutting points were designated for a low, middle, and high socioeconomic status. The largest number of cases were placed in the lower socioeconomic category, since all population studies have shown more women to have a lower social and economic status. (For example, female-headed households account for almost 40 percent of those

TABLE 2-2 *Socioeconomic Index: Sum of Scores on Education, Source, and Amount of Family Income*

SCORE	NUMBER	PERCENT
2	8	5.3
3	13	8.7
4	17	11.3
5	21	14.0
6	33	22.0
7	18	12.0
8	17	11.3
9	15	10.0
10	8	5.3

below the poverty line; Acker, 1973, p. 177.) Thus, scores of 2–5, 6–7, and 8–10 were combined. Based on this 59 women have a low status, 51 middle, and 40 high. One could dispute such a decision and argue for using equal intervals of 2–4, 5–7, 8–10 which would give 38, 72, and 40 cases in each of the three designated socioeconomic levels. Yet the logic of the earlier analysis of the reality of more women being located in the lower end of the socioeconomic scale seemed to be more compelling.

Race. This is a predominantly white study group, although 32 of the women are black. Five Puerto Rican women and one Asian woman were classified as "other." For most of the analyses, we first cross-tabulated all the 150 women by the three groups and then always dropped the category of "other" since such a small number of cases could easily distort significant relationships. We then also combined "other" with the black and then the white women.

Age. Age has been identified as an important variable in many studies of problem drinkers (Cahalan and Room, 1974). It was used as a key background variable in the present study and is based on four age groups: those under 30, those 30 to 39, those 40 to 49, and those 50 or over.

Marital status. Marital status was categorized as: married (currently living with husband), separated, divorced, widow, never married.

Religion. There was a tripartite classification of religion: Protestant, Catholic, and "other." The latter group, composed of only 14 of the women, consisted of eight Jewish women, five women who had no specific religious affiliation, and one woman who was a member of an Eastern religion. As with race, this variable was run twice: by the full complement of 150 women and then dropping the 14 women from the analysis to determine if the significant relationship continued or if a significant relationship existed when this category was omitted. The category also was combined with each of the two larger religious groups.

The two additional variables discussed below, not clearly demographic, were also viewed as important independent variables.

The Study Design: Methodology and Analysis Plan 19

Entry treatment agency (inpatient, outpatient, AA). All women were initially classified by the type of treatment setting from which they were selected: inpatient, outpatient, Alcoholics Anonymous (AA). Alcoholics Anonymous was generally viewed as conceptually similar to other outpatient women since they were not currently institutionalized or removed from their community. The women selected from the AA groups are shown separately in the analysis; like race and religion, this variable was examined by the omission of AA or the combining of AA with the other categories to determine if this smaller group was affecting the findings.

Usual quantity of drinks. The conceptualization of this variable is discussed extensively in Chapter 3 where we examine patterns of drinking. Four heavy drinking categories were evolved and form a continuum from low-heavy to very heavy drinkers.

The number of cases in each category of the ten independent variables just discussed are summarized in Table 2–3. Essentially all of the analyses for the study involved the cross-tabulation of each major dependent variable by these ten background variables.

DEPENDENT VARIABLES

To our own study group we have applied questions from a wide variety of previous research studies with alcoholics or problem drinkers. Cahalan, Cisin, and Crossley's *American Drinking Practices* (1969) provides the basis for many of our own questions on drinking practices. For example, to assess the reasons for drinking, we administered an escapist-social drinking scale (Cahalan, Cisin, and Crossley, 1969). To measure troubles attributed to drinking we reviewed previously published studies extensively. At the time the interview schedule for the present study was in process, the most exhaustive study available using the concept of troubles was found in Edwards et al. (1972). Many new items, however, were developed for the present study of women.

Certain scales that had been previously applied to other population groups were also used. To assess any possible changes in emotional status, we used Langner's 22-item scale (1962) in both the initial interview and the follow-up. Other scales were used only in the follow-up.

TABLE 2-3 *Independent Variables: Frequency Distribution*

Locale
Suburban (N=62)
Urban   (N=88)

Professional employment
Yes (N=40)
No   (N=110)

Marital and employment status
Married–employed   (N=15)
Married–not employed   (N=32)
Not married–employed   (N=38)
Not married–not employed (N=65)

Socioeconomic status (SES)
Low   (N=59)
Middle (N=51)
High   (N=40)

Race
White (N=112)
Black (N=32)
Other (N=6)

Age
Under 30 (N=27)
30–39   (N=40)
40–49   (N=50)
Over 50   (N=33)

Marital status
Married   (N=47)
Separated   (N=17)
Divorced   (N=29)
Widowed   (N=16)
Never married (N=41)

Religion
Protestant (N=66)
Catholic   (N=70)
Other   (N=14)

Agency status
Inpatient (N=73)
Outpatient (N=54)
AA   (N=23)

Usual quantity of drinks
Very heavy (15 or more drinks) (N=38)
Heavy (12–14 drinks)   (N=27)
Moderately heavy (5–11 drinks) (N=60)
Low-heavy (Less than 5 drinks) (N=25)

SINGLE-VARIABLE ANALYSIS

The limitations of single-variable analysis seem to be fairly evident; even though a significant relationship is found between two variables, there is a seemingly endless number of variables that can be crosstabulated. The selection of the variables depends not only on previous knowledge but on the thinking and judgment of the researcher concerning what is and is not important. Introducing a third explanatory variable into the analysis usually results in cells too small for a meaningful discussion. Yet when one is seeking relationships between variables and the identification of significant variables, there is no adequate substitute for such an approach to the analysis, and hypotheses must be tested in this fashion.

Because it is likely that some of the ten background variables just described are related to each other, each of these variables is crosstabulated with all the other variables and the results are discussed. Thus, when we describe "professional" women, the reader will know we are speaking primarily of women who are more likely to possess certain characteristics than the other study women, such as being white, better educated, and of a higher socioeconomic status.

SIGNIFICANCE LEVEL AND STATISTICAL ANALYSIS

A level of .05 was considered an acceptable level at which to report a significant relationship existing between variables. Those statistical relationships that are less are shown as either .01 or .001 to designate the probability of a chance occurrence. Because the present study is descriptive and exploratory, we sometimes point to important relationships on a higher significance level by using such language as a "tendency" for significance and noting either the higher probability level or the lack of the accepted significance level. Most usually, differences in the tables beyond the .05 level are indicated as not significant (NS).

Much of the data in this study are at a nominal level, but on occasion they have been transformed to an interval scale by assigning a score of "1" to indicate the presence of a variable and a score of "0" to indicate the "absence" of a variable. Also, for some of the data it has been possible to compute means and to carry out an analysis of variance to determine if there is a significant difference between means when the ten background variables described earlier are applied.

The ten background variables will now be discussed in order of frequency with which significant relationships occur with each of the other background variables. Before we begin our discussion, however, we caution the reader that most of these significant relationships between the background variables are quite weak. Using Cramer's V (as discussed in Appendix B) for most of the data, we find the strength of the relationships to be mostly on the order of .2, .3, and .4. There are several exceptions; most notable is the relatively stronger relationship between professional status and socioeconomic status (.574); the existence of a stronger relationship between marital status and the combined marital and outside employment status variable (.591) is, of course, the result of the inclusion of the one variable in the other category. Appendix B includes additional notes on the statistical procedures used in the study.

RELATIONSHIP OF MAJOR BACKGROUND VARIABLES TO EACH OTHER

Age. The relationship of the ten background variables to each other is shown in Table 2–4. There is a significant relationship between age and *one* other variable, marital status, and this is in the expected direction. As the women increase in age, they are more likely to be married, widowed, separated, or divorced. More of the younger women, less than 30 years, are likely to have never married. Relationships between two other variables, the quantity the women drink and their agency status, are of interest. Based on the four categories of age, an almost significant relationship was found by the quantity the women drink ($p < .10$). When age is dichotomized into those under and over 40, this relationship becomes significant ($p < .01$). The women under 40 are more likely to be found in the heavy and very heavy drinking categories (57 percent) while the women 40 years and over are more likely to be low heavy or moderately heavy drinkers (68 percent). When the AA women are omitted, a relationship exists between age and type of agency. This is accounted for by the women between 30 and 39 years of age, considerably more of whom (84 percent) are on an inpatient service. When the AA women are combined with the outpatient women, no relationship exists between age and type of treatment agency.

TABLE 2-4 Relationship of Major Independent Variables to Each Other

	AGE	QUANTITY OF DRINKS	RELIGION[a]	AGENCY[b]	LOCALE	MARITAL & OUTSIDE EMPLOYMENT STATUS	SOCIO-ECONOMIC STATUS	MARITAL STATUS	RACE[c]	PROFESSIONAL EMPLOYMENT
Age	—	NS	NS	NS	NS	NS	NS	<.05	NS	NS
Quantity of drinks	NS	—	NS	NS	<.001	NS	NS	NS	NS	NS
Religion[a]	NS	NS	—	NS	NS	NS	<.05[a]	NS	<.001	<.05
Agency[b]	NS	NS	NS	—	NS	<.01	<.01	NS	NS	<.01
Locale	NS	<.001	NS	NS	—	<.001	NS	<.001	<.001	NS
Marital & outside employment status	NS	NS	NS	<.01	<.001	—	<.001	<.001	<.001	<.001
Socioeconomic status	NS	NS	<.05	<.01	NS	<.001	—	<.001	<.001	<.001
Marital status	<.05	NS	NS	NS	<.001	<.001	<.001	—	<.05	<.01
Race[c]	NS	NS	<.001	NS	<.001	<.01	<.001	<.05	—	<.01
Professional employment	NS	NS	<.05	<.01	NS	<.001	<.001	<.01	<.01	—

[a] *Religion*: When the category of "other" (N=14) is eliminated or combined with either Protestant or Catholic, the significant relationship between socioeconomic status and religion and professional status by religion disappears, but race persists as significant.
[b] *Agency*: When the AA women (N=23) are omitted from the computations, the significant relationships disappear, but age becomes significant. When the AA women are combined with other outpatients, the lack of a significant relationship persists. Thus, the significant relationship is accounted for by the AA members.
[c] *Race*: Dropping the small category of "other" (N=6) from the analysis does not affect any of the significant relationships reported, nor does combining the "other" with either the white or black women.

Usual quantity of drinks. This variable is related to *one* of the other variables: urban-suburban residence. Just over four-fifths of the very heavy drinkers (15 or more drinks) are from the urban area and almost two-thirds of the moderately heavy drinkers (5–11 drinks) are from suburban areas. As we just noted, when only two categories of age are used, more of the very heavy and heavy drinkers are under 40 years.

Religion. Religion is related to *three* other variables: socioeconomic status, race, and professional status. Two of the significant relationships, professional status and socioeconomic status, are the result of the smaller category of "other" and significant findings do not persist when this category is omitted or combined with each of the two larger categories. Thus, professional women are found in similar proportions in the Protestant and Catholic groups, and the significant difference is accounted for by the smaller category of "other" women. The Protestant and Catholic women are similarly distributed in the three SES groups, and it is only the smaller group of "other" women who account for the significant relationship. Just more than half (57 percent) of the Protestant women are white, more than four-fifths (86 percent) of the Catholic women are white, and all of the smaller group of women designated as "other" in their religious affiliation are also white. This significant relationship of religion by race persists when the category of "other" is omitted from the analysis, or when it is combined.

Entry treatment agency (inpatient, outpatient, AA). Three variables are significantly related to the type of agency: marital and outside employment status, socioeconomic group, and professional status. All three relationships disappear when the smaller number of AA women are eliminated from the analysis. Age is close ($p < .06$) to significance but becomes significant ($p < .05$) when AA women are omitted. Outpatients, including AA women, are more likely to be under 30. Almost two-thirds of the AA women are under 40: This is true for only one-third of the other outpatients and one-half of the inpatients. Both inpatient and outpatient settings have fairly similar proportions of women over 50.

The Study Design: Methodology and Analysis Plan 25

Locale: Urban or suburban place of residence. The women's residence is related to four other variables: the quantity the women drink, the combination of marital and outside employment status, marriage, and race. The quantity the women drink is significantly related to their place of residence with 56 percent of the urban women in the heavy or very heavy categories and 74 percent of the suburban women in the moderately heavy or low-heavy categories of drinking. For the marital and outside employment variable, the largest percentage of suburban women can be found in the married-not employed category (40 percent) and similarly the highest percentage of urban women are not married and not employed (51 percent). More than half of the suburban women are currently married (55 percent), with 25 percent separated or divorced, 10 percent widowed, and only 10 percent never having married. In contrast, only 15 percent of the urban women are currently married, 34 percent are now separated or divorced, 11 percent are widowed, and 40 percent never married. The suburban women are predominantly white (94 percent), whereas just under two-thirds of the urban women are white.

Marital and outside employment status. To this complex variable, which comprises four separate categories (currently married and employed, currently married and not employed; not currently married and employed, not currently married and not employed), six other variables are significantly related: agency, urban-suburban residence, socioeconomic status, marriage, race, and professional status. The significant relationship between this variable and the type of agency is primarily due to the large number of married and employed women in AA (47 percent). Significance does not persist when AA is omitted as a category or combined with outpatients. The urban-suburban women show a significant relationship between their marital and employment status; 78 percent of the married and not employed women live in suburbs, while 79 percent of the not currently married but employed women live in urban areas. The married and employed women are mostly in the middle to upper socioeconomic categories. Relatively the same pattern is found for the married and unemployed women. Those who are not currently married but employed are distributed in a similar fashion to the married and employed women. It is those who are not currently married and not employed who are in the lower socioeconomic group. A significant relationship exists, as expected, between marital status and this combination variable. The currently not-married women who are employed are primarily the never-married women (47 percent) and account for more women than those separated, divorced, or widowed. The first three categories of this variable are dominated by between 80 percent to 90 percent of the white women. In the latter category of not married and not employed are 57 percent of the white women and 35 percent of the black women. The professional women are located in larger numbers in the married and employed and the not currently married but employed groups.

Socioeconomic status (SES). This variable was significantly related to six other background variables: religion, agency, marital and outside employment status, marriage, race, and professional status. The relationship between socioeconomic status and religion is accounted for by the "other" in religion. More than half of the women in each SES category are inpatients; the significant relationship between this variable and the entry agency disappears when the AA women are omitted from the analysis since more than one-third of the high SES category consists of AA women. The significant relationship between marital and outside employment status and socioeconomic status is a result of the low SES category in which 78 percent of the women are not married and not employed. Almost two-thirds of the not married, both employed and not employed, are in the middle-income group. The high-income group is dominated by the married and not employed women (38 percent) and the not married and employed women (40 percent). By marital status, just half of the high socioeconomic group is married, while another 40 percent are in the never-married category. The middle-income group shows just over a third of the women to be currently married and almost another third divorced. The low-income group has a fairly equal distribution in all five of the marital status categories; slightly more of the never-married women (29 percent) are found in this low-income group, and slightly fewer of the married (14 percent) are also found here. Almost all of the high socioeconomic group is white; more than half of the low socioeconomic group consists of white women with just over a third black. The high socioeconomic group is composed of more than two-thirds of the professional women, with the lower socioeconomic group containing only 5 percent of the professional women.

Marital status. This variable is related to six of the other variables: age, urban-suburban residence, marital and outside employment status, socioeconomic status, race, and professional women. As might be expected, a majority of the widows are older; 87 percent are over 40; most of the separated and divorced women are in the 30-year-old to 49-year-old group. The married women are primarily over 30 (89 percent), while more than one-third of the never-married women are under 30. The married women are most likely (72 percent) to live in the suburban areas and those who were never married (85 percent) in the urban areas. A majority of the separated, widowed, and divorced women also live in the urban areas. The variable of marital and outside employment status shows just over three-fourths of the separated and widowed women are not employed. Just about two-fifths of the married and never-married women are in the high socioeconomic group. The women who are separated or widowed account for somewhat more than two-thirds of the women in the lower socioeconomic group. Almost 90 percent of the married women are white; in only two categories did the white and black women appear in fairly similar proportions: separated and widowed. A preponderance of the never-married women (73 percent) are white. Almost half (46 percent) of the never-married women are professional women.

Race. Race is related to six other variables: religion, urban-suburban residence, marital and outside employment status, socioeconomic status, marriage, and professional status. Just over half of the white women (54 percent) are Catholic, and the black women are predominantly Protestant (88 percent). The white women are almost equally likely to be found in the suburban areas as in the urban areas; in sharp contrast, almost all (91 percent) of the black women are from the urban communities. The majority of both groups of white and black women appear in the group of those women who are not currently married, whether employed or not, but the black women are considerably more likely (72 percent) not to be employed and not to be married when compared to the white women in this category (33 percent). Almost equal proportions of the white women are found in the low, middle, and high socioeconomic groups; two-thirds of the black women are in the lower income group, almost a third in the middle, and 3 percent in the higher. More than one-third of the white women are currently married as compared to 16 percent of the black women. Similar proportions of white and black women are in the category of never married—just over one-fourth. While 34 percent of the white women are professional women, only 6 percent of the black women are professionals. There is a close to significant relationship ($p < .06$) between race and the type of agency when the smaller category of "other" in race is omitted. One-fifth of the white women entered the study from AA, while this is the case for less than 4 percent of the black women. This difference is probably related to our selection process as well as the reported lower proportion of black women in AA.

Professional employment. Six variables have a statistically significant relationship with the women's professional employment: religion, agency, marital and outside employment status, socioeconomic status, marital status, and race. Also, the urban-suburban variable borders on significance ($p < .06$). The statistical significance of religion is accounted for primarily by the category of "other" with 14 cases. Once the "other" is dropped from the analysis, the relationship between religion and professional employment is not significant. The significant relationship with the type of agency is accounted for by almost a third of the professional women coming from AA groups. Once AA is eliminated from the analysis, the significant relationship disappears. The combination variable of married and employed shows 53 percent of the professional women in the not-married-but-employed category. A preponderance of the professional women are at the upper end of the scale with scores reflecting higher socioeconomic status; this accounts for more than two-thirds of the professional women. Also, professional women are primarily currently married, or they were never married. Relatively few are divorced, widowed, or separated. The professional employment of this group of respondents is significantly related to race since 95 percent of the study's population of professional women are white. The urban-suburban variable, which is found to be close to significant, is the result of 73 percent of the professional women coming from urban areas.

Note
1. The scales included in the follow-up interview were: anomie, self-esteem, and androgyny.

3
Patterns of Drinking

Summary of findings

The average age at which the study women started drinking was 21.

Problem drinking began on the average at age 33, an average of 12 years after drinking first started. Problem drinking started earliest (age 30) for women never married, latest (age 40) for women who are widowed.

Over one-half of the women sought treatment within 5 years of the start of problem drinking, typically at age 38.

Urban women drink greater quantities of alcohol, the urban nonprofessional women being the heaviest drinkers. The average amount consumed daily by the study women is slightly more than 11 drinks. Women who usually drink less than five drinks per day all have a history of heavier drinking, although most do not exceed five-to-seven drinks.

Two-thirds of the women drink daily; 28 percent are binge drinkers.

Over one-half of the women had never had more to drink than in the week prior to entry into treatment; over one-half describe the year prior to the research interview as their most typical period of heavy drinking.

Women are more likely to drink hard liquor than wine or beer.

Eighty-four percent of the women most often drink in their own homes.

More of the employed women drink fairly often in restaurants and bars. Professional women drink more often in restaurants and bars than nonprofessional women, and white women more often than black women. Catholic women drink more often in restaurants and bars than do Protestant women. Women of higher socioeconomic status do more restaurant and bar drinking than do those of lower socioeconomic status.

Married women (employed or not) and employed women who are not married account for the bulk of women who drink alone. The higher the socioeconomic status of a woman, the more likely she is to drink alone.

Women categorized as very heavy drinkers are most likely to state they would miss drinking "a lot" if they gave it up entirely.

Twenty-two percent of the study women do not know *anyone* in their neighborhood.

Almost two-thirds of the women who know people in their neighborhood know heavy-drinking women; 40 percent of these women report that these neighbors have not had help for their drinking problems.

Professional and single-and-employed women are less likely to know their neighbors and, if they do, are less likely to know people who drink heavily; unemployed women (married or not) are more likely to know heavy-drinking neighbors and to drink with others.

Over one-half of the women drink with people from their neighborhood but tend, in general, to drink less than usual when with neighbors, co-workers, and family members. They tend to abstain when with people from their church and are most likely to drink the same as usual only when with close friends.

Sixty-one percent of the women have close friends with a drinking problem; 20 percent of them believe that the friendship has resulted in an increase in their own drinking.

Two-thirds of the women do something to hide their drinking; more suburban and married women hide their drinking, and more of the suburban professional women hide their drinking when compared with the other women. The higher the socioeconomic status of the woman the more likely she is to hide her drinking. The greater the quantity of liquor consumed, the less likely is the woman to hide her drinking.

Most women offer escapist rather than social reasons for drinking. Black women are more likely to give a social reason for drinking, and women under age 30 are more likely to give an escapist reason.

Fifty-one percent of the women reported that problem drinking was preceded by some specific pressure; pressures most frequently mentioned were described as psychological losses.

Almost equally large percentages of the women believe they persist in their drinking either because of an affective or feeling state such as being unhappy, lonely, anxious, or depressed or because of the effects alcohol produces. Those *not* drinking because of their feeling state are more likely to be drinking for the effect. If a woman states she is maintaining her drinking because of a specific life situation, she is less likely to be drinking for the effect.

Almost one-half of the women have used other drugs *while drinking;* 42 percent of all subjects who have used other drugs have used tranquilizers or sedatives, 24 percent have used sleeping pills, and 15 percent have used stimulants while drinking.

Eighty-two percent have used other drugs in addition to alcohol, while not necessarily simultaneously, at some time in their lives. The use of other drugs is greatest by the white women, those under age 30, and those categorized as very heavy drinkers.

White women, subjects under age 30, and very heavy drinkers are also most likely to use other drugs *while drinking*.

White women are more likely to use other depressants and/or stimulants while drinking than are black women; there are no racial differences in the use of opiates, cocaine, or hallucinogens while drinking.

Those who drink very heavy amounts of alcohol (15 or more drinks) and those under 30 seem to run a considerably higher risk than the other women of experiencing the lethal effects of taking alcohol and other drugs in combination.

Numerous studies have attempted to deal with the drinking patterns of alcoholic women. The findings have often been conflicting and generalizations difficult. The current study examines the patterns of drinking within the context of the major demographic variables described in the previous chapter. This present chapter describes the age at the onset of drinking and of problem drinking in women as compared with those of men, the pressures for drinking, and the quantity and frequency of drinking. Included is a description of the type of alcohol consumed, the setting and situation of drinking, and the extent of drinking among friends and neighbors. Secrecy in drinking and the existence of social or escapist reasons for drinking are also examined. Finally, assessment is made of the use of other drugs in addition to alcohol and the reasons given by the women for the maintenance of drinking.

Onset of drinking and problem drinking

Studies of female alcoholics consistently report an older mean age for the time of the first drink than do studies of male alcoholics (Johnson et al., 1966; Kinsey, 1966; Rimmer et al., 1971). Lisansky (1957) found that the alcoholic women in her study first started drinking at age 20.8, while the men started drinking at age 17 ($p < .01$). The women in the present study first started drinking between the ages of 5 and 51, the average being 20.6 years of age.[1] Obviously this age is remarkably similar to Lisansky's study of more than two decades ago and is consistent with those of earlier studies of women, all of which indicates that the present generation of alcoholic women generally begin drinking somewhat later than do alcoholic men. Because of the increasing social equality between women and men, the present observation of a later age at which women begin drinking will probably not hold in future studies of alcoholic women.

Norms for the age at which women in the general population begin to drink by the age groups used in the present study are not readily available. Yet, evidence increasingly indicates that there is little difference in drinking behavior by gender at the younger age ranges. For example, in the mid-1970s, 93 percent of the boys and 87 percent of the girls began their drinking by the 12th grade (United States Department of Health, Education, and Welfare, 1974, *Alcohol and Health*, p. 8).

Telescoped drinking

The term "telescoping" has been used to describe what appears to be a more rapid progression of alcoholism in women. As Lisansky (1957, p. 608) points out when discussing telescoping, two separate periods can be distinguished: first, the period in which there is "the shift from abstinence or moderate drinking to alcoholism, a shift which theoretically could take place overnight or could take several years"; second, the period in which the individual person continues problem drinking until seen at a clinic or hospital. "What has been demonstrated in this and other studies is that the latter period is shorter for alcoholic women than it is for alcoholic men . . . The interval between the shift from abstinence or moderate drinking to problem drinking needs study."

Let us discuss first this transition from moderate to problem drinking. The age at which drinking begins seems to affect the age at which problem drinking emerges. Most studies that present data on the onset of problem drinking report that women, on the average, become problem drinkers at a later age than men. For example, the men in Lisansky's study (1957) began drinking heavily at age 27.3, while the women began at age 31.4 ($p < .02$). Twenty years later Mulford (1977), using a somewhat different concept (that is, "problem drinking" rather than "heavy drinking"), gave a similar report. In his study, the women were more than two years older than the men at the onset of problem drinking, 34.7 as compared to 32.5 years. Onset of problem drinking before the age of 25 occurred for 23 percent of the men, but for only 16 percent of the women. The age of onset of problem drinking in women ranges from 30 to 39 (Glatt, 1961; Winokur, et al., 1970). The reported range for men is from 27.3 to 32.5 (Lisansky, 1957; Mulford, 1977). In the present study, after first starting to drink on the average at age 21, about 12 years passed on the average before the women began to worry about their drinking and to perceive it as a problem. Thus the average (mean) age of the beginning of problem drinking is 33 for the study women. More will be said about the variation in the age of onset of problem drinking later.

In the absence of data in our study on men from the same treatment settings, it is not possible to draw firm conclusions on the existence of telescoping of the interval between moderate and problem drinking. The women in the present study drank an average of twelve years before beginning to perceive drinking as a problem, while men *and* women in Lisansky's (1957) study began drinking heavily an average of ten years after first starting to drink. While it is clear that further controlled research is needed in this area, the findings from this study and Lisansky's raise questions about the existence of a telescoped time span between moderate and problem drinking for women. Most probably, any differences found between men and women are the result of the later age at which women begin their drinking.

The age of onset of problem drinking by women in our study varied only by marital status and was unrelated to the other background variables, including current age. Study women who have never been married report problem drinking starting at age 30, while women currently living with spouses, separated, or divorced report problems associated with drinking beginning several years later. Women who are widowed report problem drinking starting at a significantly later age, on the average not until age 40 ($p < .05$). Before examining the data, we thought that the later age for onset could be related to the death of a husband, but this proved not to be the case. Of the sixteen widows in the study, five traced the onset of problem drinking to the death of their husband. The others also had a later age for onset of problem drinking, but this onset *preceded* the husband's death.

The second aspect of telescoping referred to by Lisansky *does appear* to exist for the present study women. The women in Lisansky's study had been problem drinkers for 9.8 years before seeking treatment as compared with 12.3 years for the men, a close to significant difference ($p < .10$). Mulford (1977) found the women in his study had been drinking heavily for a shorter period of time before entering treatment, 3.7 years compared to 6.5 years for men. This earlier help-seeking behavior by women has been reported by innumerable investigators in American, British, and Australian publications (Winokur and Clayton, 1968; Wilkinson et al., 1969; Schuckit et al., 1969; Wanberg and Knapp, 1970b; Sclare, 1970). Wanberg and Knapp (1970b), for example, found that while women alcoholics begin drinking heavily at a significantly later age than men, they are hospitalized at about the same age.

After beginning to perceive their drinking as a problem, the women in the present study sought treatment an average of 6 years later: 28 percent within 1 year, 28 percent between 2 to 5 years, 24 percent from 6 to 15 years, and only 9 percent waited over 15 years before seeking help for their drinking. Data were not available for 11 percent of the study women.

Information from other studies on the time elapsing before treatment is sought provides some basis for comparisons between women and men. The 6-year period between problem drinking and treatment reported in our present study falls between Mulford's (1977)—3.7 years—and Lisansky's (1957)—9.8 years. While it is substantially less than the 12.3 years reported for the men in Lisansky's study, it is almost identical to the 6.5 years reported for men in Mulford's population. Yet, in the absence of data on men from the same treatment settings, it is not possible to look to this data for support of the existence of "telescoping" between problem drinking and treatment in women. The different time spans in the studies cited may well be attributed to the number of years between the two studies and to the different geographic location of the Mulford study group as well as to differences in the background of the women studied. What seems most important is that considerable time still elapses before the women in this study entered treatment.

Pressures for drinking

After determining when drinking became a problem for the study women, an attempt was then made to establish if there were any special problems or pressures surrounding the beginning of a drinking problem. As noted earlier, studies relating to women with a drinking problem have tended to point to a precipitating event transforming moderate social drinking into problem drinking. This facet of the development of problem drinking in women has been discussed in most reviews of the literature on women (Gomberg, 1974; Corrigan, 1974b; Beckman, 1975). Oddly enough, this aspect has not been especially emphasized in studies of problem drinking by men. Such an explanation may well be an oversimplification of the complex process of alcoholism; those writing about men may have had less need to justify what they thought was expected and found acceptable. The expectation, based on earlier research on women, that most of the women in the present study would acknowledge a specific event precipitating their problem drinking was not confirmed. While 51 percent reported problem drinking had been preceded by some special pressure, 49 percent could not point to any specific pressures or event. Yet when a specific incident was cited, those most frequently mentioned were marital problems or death (26 percent and 28 percent respectively). Most of the other precipitating situations cited also involved "losses." Thus, a *marital problem* could be viewed as the loss of a "love" relationship; *death* most clearly is the ultimate loss; *illnesses or accidents* (11 percent) have sometimes been viewed in the context of a loss of self-esteem or precipitating anxiety about a loss of life. *Moving* to another neighborhood (5 percent) has also been amply documented as an uprooting experience, one that involves a loss of associations, especially for women. Some women—but relatively few—cited an unwanted pregnancy, loss of job, menopause, or abortion (ranging between 1 percent and 3 percent) as a precipitating life situation. It would seem that all these life events fit within the framework of a psychological loss.

Such losses are also frequently cited in the literature as a precipitating event in depression. Alcoholic women, too, are often found to present depressive symptoms, but a distinction is made between depressive symptoms resulting from alcohol acting as a depressant and the primary diagnosis of depression with alcohol as an additional problem (Schuckit and Morrissey, 1976). This, of course, is not the first time that depression and the onset of problem drinking have been associated. Yet, this remains an unsatisfactory explanation for the etiology of alcoholism in women since a multitude of women experiencing similar life "losses" have not become alcoholic.

Many study women did not identify a specific critical situation but nonetheless pointed to a variety of situational problems with which they often felt they could not cope. For example, one young woman "hated home," ran away, and was arrested as a wayward minor. Thereafter she started to drink more heavily. Still another woman said that when she began heavy drinking she was concerned about her daughter and husband; she also had financial worries. Loneliness was cited by relatively few women, but when mentioned, it was most usually connected with a husband's long hours of work. It seems fairly clear that specific pressures exist for a subgroup of alcoholic women, and there is recognition of problem drinking following specific life events, most usually emotional losses. Yet almost as many women could not identify any pressure for problem drinking. Whether or not two groups of alcoholic women can indeed be distinguished on this basis may be an area for future study.

Alcohol consumption

The measurement of alcohol consumption has been refined in the last decade for the general population. Cahalan, Cisin, and Crossley (1969) described the drinking practices of Americans by identifying the proportions who are total abstainers as well as infrequent, light, moderate, and heavy drinkers. They report that 77 percent of the men and 60 percent of the women drink at least once a year; of those who drink, 28 percent of the men and 8 percent of the women were classified as heavy drinkers.

It is primarily the heavy drinkers who are of the greatest interest in a study of a treated population. Studies of treated populations cannot use the standard categories of the Quantity-Frequency-Variability (Q-F-V) index as applied to a general population since the drinking of a treated group will often be beyond five or more drinks.[2] Yet a measure of variability in the quantity consumed among heavy-drinking women was viewed as important for a number of reasons. It was assumed that there would be a wide range in the quantity of alcohol consumed by women with drinking problems and this variation would serve as an important independent variable when measuring the effects of drinking. A major difference in the quantity consumed was expected between women and men because of the difference in body weight and the differing mind set about drinking. Nonetheless, there was obviously a need to reconceptualize consumption and to offer a more precise measurement. An observation by Room (1968) seems

Patterns of Drinking

most germane: "Some who are labeled as alcoholic drink less than is common in the general population." He also notes that "virtually there are no detailed reports of how much those labeled as alcoholic drink, of what and how often." Such reports are only beginning to emerge.

In Room's analysis of available data of institutionalized alcoholics, a smaller proportion of women consistently drink a pint or more on a regular basis; roughly about a fourth of the women drink a half-pint or less, compared to 10 percent of the men. At the other end of the spectrum, a considerably smaller percentage of women are likely to drink more than two pints—less than 5 percent as compared to approximately 22 percent of the men.[3] Thus Room's data point to a significant proportion of men and women alcoholics drinking substantially the same quantity but a sizable segment of the women drinking less. In the present study, we asked detailed information about the time each woman had the *most* to drink. A card (see below) with the equivalent volume of each beverage by its amount of alcohol was

	Spirits—whiskey, hard liquor, gin, rum, brandy, etc.	Beer or ale	Sherry, port, vermouth, muscatel or other sweet wines	Other table wines, rosé, dry wines
A	1 quart or more— 21 drinks or more	7 quarts or 19 cans or over	2 bottles or more (either quarts or fifths)	1 gallon or more
B	1 fifth or 15–20 drinks	6 quarts or 16–18 cans	1½ bottles (either quarts or fifths)	3 bottles (either quarts or fifths)
C	1 pint or 12–14 drinks	5 quarts or 13–15 cans	1 bottle (either quart or fifth)	2 bottles (either quarts or fifths)
D	¾ pint or 8–11 drinks	4 quarts or 10–12 cans	¾ bottle (either quart or fifth)	1½ bottles (either quarts or fifths)
E	½ pint or 5–7 drinks	3 quarts or 7–9 cans	1 pint or ½ a quart or fifth	1 bottle (either quart or fifth)

handed to each woman and she was asked to state which of the following "best describes how much you had to drink on that occasion."[4]

> Amount A equivalent of 21 or more drinks
> B " 15–20 drinks
> C " 12–14 "
> D " 8–11 "
> E " 5–7 "

The next questions related to the frequency with which they drank these amounts when they had the most to drink. The following table shows the quantity consumed nearly every day or one to three times weekly on such occasions. Only shown are those women who drank these amounts nearly every day or one to three times weekly. Omitted are those who drank these same amounts less frequently and those who drank less than five drinks daily, Table 3–1.

Almost three-fourths (72 percent) of the women drank these amounts nearly every day with two-fifths drinking 15 or more drinks daily. Somewhat fewer, about two-thirds drank these amounts one to three times weekly. The other women were binge or weekend drinkers, or those who drank less than five drinks daily. Binge drinking will be discussed shortly.

Next, the quantity the women *usually drink daily* was examined separately. Since 21 women did not drink daily, each of these cases

TABLE 3–1 *Study Women Who Usually Drink More Than Five Drinks Daily or One to Three Times Weekly: Percentage Distribution*

NUMBER OF DRINKS[a]	NEARLY EVERY DAY (N=108)	ONE-THREE TIMES WEEKLY (N=101)
21	26	15
15–20	13	22
12–14	20	21
8–11	26	21
5–7	15	21

[a] Three women did not answer this question and four stated that binge drinking occurred less frequently than once per week. The remaining women drank less than five drinks.

was individually reviewed. These nondaily drinkers are mostly binge or weekend drinkers. They were subsequently classified according to the amount they drink on the occasion of their drinking. The final scheme used to reflect the quantity the women usually drinks is shown in Table 3–2. Thus, when they are drinking, more than four-fifths (83 percent) of the women studied consume five or more drinks. In fact, a substantial percentage consume a considerable quantity, with 25 percent drinking the equivalent of a fifth of alcohol.

These four categories are those used throughout the study to refer to the usual quantity the women drink. An obvious question raised by these data relates to the lowest volume consumed, less than five drinks. This group, too, obviously represents a substantial proportion of the women (17 percent) who see themselves as having a drinking problem. It will be recalled that approximately 10 percent of the institutionalized women described by Room consume this smaller quantity (1968).

In the present study, when asked about the most they have to drink, a majority reported heavier drinking. Yet three-fifths of those usually consuming less than five drinks reported not exceeding five to seven drinks when asked about the most they have to drink. Those who claimed to drink this higher amount do so at least several times a month, but more typically several times a week.

These data serve to reinforce and dramatize what may or may not be known. The *usual* amount a person drinks is insufficient to portray an understanding of alcohol consumption; frequency of drinking is an added piece of datum that is needed. What may be of even greater importance for women is to determine quantity and frequency during periods of heaviest drinking. This is likely to be a more accurate ap-

TABLE 3–2 *Usual Quantity Consumed When Drinking: Percentage Distribution*

NUMBER OF DRINKS	(N=150)	QUANTITY
15 or more drinks	25	Very heavy
12–14	18	Heavy
5–11	40	Moderately heavy
Less than 5	17	Low-heavy

proach for clinicians and others to use in assessing the nature of women's drinking problems, especially for those who seem to drink less than what is expected of an alcoholic woman.

The average amount consumed daily by the study women is slightly more than 11 drinks or a pint of spirits each day. What may possibly surprise some readers is that more urban women than suburban women reported themselves as usually drinking greater quantities of alcohol ($p < .001$). While over one-third of the urban women stated they usually have 15 or more drinks daily, only 11 percent of the suburban women reported drinking this quantity. Most of the suburban women can be considered moderately heavy (5–11 drinks) or low-heavy drinkers (less than 5 drinks), while a majority of the urban women are in the very heavy (15 or more drinks) or heavy (12–14 drinks) categories of drinking. No other background variable is found to be significant. Substantial differences do emerge among the women when the area of residence is controlled and professional status introduced. Of the 38 women found to be very heavy drinkers, 66 percent are urban women who are not in a professional occupation.

Over one-half of the study women described the year prior to the interview as their most typical period of heavy drinking. In the week prior to entering treatment, those women who were drinking had consumed an average of 69 drinks per person, or very close to the average of 11 drinks daily. In addition, over one-half of the study women stated that the amount they had to drink in this week prior to entering treatment is as much as they had ever had to drink.

A discussion of the validity, that is, accuracy, and reliability, the consistency, of this global approach to measuring the quantity of alcohol consumed is appropriate here. Some may wonder about the vagaries of recall in the questions as they relate to "most to drink," "usual amount," or even the accuracy of recalling consumption in the week prior to entering treatment. Some may even wonder if women are less likely than male alcoholics to report accurately the quantity and frequency of their alcohol consumption. Other researchers have dealt with these concerns, and since their reasoning is compelling, we call on it here (Cahalan, Cisin, and Crossley, 1969, pp. 11–12).

The problem of measuring beverage consumption and classifying people according to amount of drinking has many facets. . . .

Many workers in the field have used some kind of quantity-frequency [Q-F] index of the amount of alcoholic beverages consumed over a period of time.

The statistical reliability of any method of measurement [that] depends on respondents' judgments of their usual behavior is limited. . . . Hence the reliability and validity of reports of usual drinking may not be high enough for precise placement of individuals on a scale. . . . A more useful tool might be exact reports of the quantity drunk in a specific, brief recent period. . . . But this procedure would catch respondents at atypical times and lead to incorrect groupings for average, usual behavior. Q-F is the most useful tool for the purpose of group comparison. Since the goal of the present survey is to describe usual behavior in terms of group differences . . . , the analysis is based upon a variant of this type of index.

Because of the nature and focus of our study, we have been most interested in the average drinking behavior of the study women, not in the most they had to drink or in what amount they consumed just prior to treatment. These two dimensions of drinking were, indeed, also obtained, and they tend to confirm the conclusion that the *usual amount* does not distort the *quantity* consumed. Rather, the major question in this study is how the usual drinking pattern of the study women—and as it turned out the variations in the quantity consumed—has affected their lives.

Binge drinkers

As noted earlier, most of the women studied are daily drinkers. There have been conflicting reports about women as binge drinkers.[5] Several studies report a smaller proportion of women than men as binge drinkers. Rimmer et al. (1971) found that 47 percent of the women and 67 percent of the men studied were binge drinkers, percentages they confirmed in a 1972 study. Madden and Jones (1972), however, found women are more likely to be binge drinkers: only 27 percent of the men in contrast to 56 percent of women. In the present study, relatively few of the women are binge drinkers, with only 28 percent describing themselves as such.

The implications of the existence of such differing drinking types—daily and weekend or binge drinkers—is not clear, either for treatment or assessment of the consequences. It is thought, however, that the period of time between binges may grow shorter and that such drinkers often become daily drinkers.

Type of alcoholic beverage

In addition to data gathered on onset and patterns of problem drinking, information was obtained on the type of alcoholic beverage used at different time periods. When the women first began to drink, 17 percent drank beer, 7 percent drank wine, 50 percent drank some type of hard liquor, and 26 percent drank a combination of beer, wine, and hard liquor. The types of liquor consumed more recently are almost identical in their percentage distribution; yet only 31 percent of the study women drank just prior to treatment the same type of beverage alcohol they drank initially. It would seem, then, that women as a group will drink the same proportion of these varying types of alcohol, while women as individuals will change the type of alcohol they consume over their lifetime of drinking. Forty percent drink an entirely different type of liquor, and 26 percent drink the type they began drinking plus another type. Also, most are more likely to drink hard liquor than wine or beer. There are significant differences ($p < .05$) by occupation. Professional women are less likely to drink beer (3 percent) and more likely to drink wine (18 percent), whereas nonprofessional women are more likely to drink a combination of beer and hard liquor. The use of hard liquor is most typical of the study women, and they are likely to be drinking a different type of liquor than when they first started drinking.

Setting and situation of drinking

It has been said that women are most likely to drink in their own homes because that is where they spend most of their time. The present study offered the opportunity to determine if women who work outside the home are also more likely to drink outside. First, the women were asked where they *most often* drink, and then *how often* they are likely to drink in their own home, with friends, or in restaurants or bars. The overwhelming majority (85 percent) reported they most often drink in their own homes. Obviously, then, the setting in which the women drink *most often* is not influenced to any extent by employment status or is there any relationship to any of the other background variables. National surveys between 1971 and 1976 show that 50 percent of heavier[6] drinking women drink at least monthly in bars and 34 percent in restaurants (Johnson et al., 1977). Information in these surveys on the drinking practices of adults in the United States does not indicate the work status of the women studied.

In the present study, it was when the women were asked *how often* they drink in a restaurant or bar that differences in their work status emerged. While not a statistically significant difference, there is a likelihood for currently working women to drink *fairly often* in restaurants and bars compared to women who are not employed, 40 percent and 26 percent respectively ($p < .08$). Almost half of the women who are *not* employed state they almost never drink in restaurants or bars. Thus the woman who is not employed more obviously fits the stereotype of the woman drinking at home. When women who have a drinking problem are employed, they are also more likely to drink outside the home.

Only three of the background variables are significantly related to the frequency of drinking in restaurants or bars: professional status, race, and religion. Professional women are more likely to drink in restaurants or bars than are nonprofessional women. While two-fifths of the professional women drink in restaurants or bars fairly often, this is the case for only 27 percent of the other women ($p < .01$). Thus the drinking behavior of working women, particularly professional women, is probably as visible and observable as that of men.

Relatively few (6 percent) of the black women in the study drink in restaurants or bars "fairly often" as compared to 38 percent of the white women in the study ($p < .001$). In addition, Catholic women, almost all of whom are white, are much more likely to drink in restaurants or bars (39 percent) than are Protestant women (18 percent, $p < .001$). The racial differences reported in restaurant or bar drinking may be accounted for by the socioeconomic variable, since the black women in this study group are more likely to be in the lower socioeconomic group and hence less able to use these settings for their drinking. Alternately, cultural constraints against this group of black women drinking in public may be greater. Of some interest is a related finding: Forty-five percent of the women in the highest socioeconomic group are most likely to drink fairly often in restaurants or bars, a close to significant difference ($p < .07$). It should be noted that this finding conflicts with those of other studies showing that women in the lowest socioeconomic groups are more likely to be bar drinkers (Cramer and Blacker, 1966).

Some provocative and interesting differences were found among the women when asked if they were *most likely* to drink alone or with someone else. Overall, 71 percent of the women say they are *most* likely to drink alone. No difference is found between women of urban and suburban residence. Rather, it is the currently married women who are most likely to drink alone, 87 percent ($p < .05$), when compared with the women who are not currently married, only 65 percent of whom report they are most likely to drink alone. These findings are consistent with those of Mulford (1977), who found married women to be more inclined toward solitary drinking. In addition, women employed outside the home are more likely to drink alone ($p < .05$). When marriage and work status are examined together, the results are highly significant ($p < .01$). With marital status controlled, it is the married women, employed or not, and the not-married working-women who account for the bulk of the women who drink alone. Only 58 percent of those neither married nor employed report they are most likely to drink alone. Yet 71 percent of the single working-women, 81 percent of the housewives (married but not working outside the home), and all of the employed married women ($N = 15$) say they most likely drink alone.

What this seems to mean is that more of those women who have a greater opportunity for contact with others, either through marriage or employment, most often drink alone. One explanation for this finding is that the women who still have strong ties to others, either through marriage or work, are more likely to shield themselves from others having knowledge of the extent of their drinking by drinking alone. In turn, women who lack these stronger affiliations have less to risk by drinking with others and are almost as likely to drink with someone else. Consistent with this interpretation is the finding that 78 percent of those in the middle and higher socioeconomic groups most likely drink alone ($p < .05$).

Of related interest is the analysis of a number of national surveys which also seems consistent with the findings reported: "women who are both married and employed have higher rates of problem drinking than housewives and single working women" (Johnson et al., 1977, p. vi). The authors offer two explanations: role conflict as wife and employee, or the conformity of the working woman to the norms of a drinking male work force (Johnson et al., 1977, p. 56). Johnson and her colleagues suggest the first explanation as a transitional phenomena, which could well be erased as the nontraditional role of working outside the home becomes traditional and accepted. They further speculate that if it is conformity to male heavy-drinking norms, then alcoholism for women is likely to increase, provided the norms for heavier drinking do not change.

Several studies report women drinking alone at home significantly more often than men (Wood and Duffy, 1966; Wanberg and Knapp, 1970). These findings have been interpreted as reflecting the "lonely housewife" who is bored at home. While the present study indicates that this may be the case with some women, there are others (that is, married and unmarried employed women) for whom this does not apply. Also, it has been noted by some (Wanberg and Horn, 1970; Wanberg and Knapp, 1970) that alcohol helps women do their daily household chores, yet only 28 percent of the subjects in the present study say they do housework when drinking alone.[7] The great majority engage in very passive activities when drinking alone; 41 percent listen to music, the radio, or watch television; and 11 percent "do nothing." Only 9 percent read when drinking alone, and relatively few talk on the telephone. In contrast to these passive pursuits of the solitary drinker, three-fourths who drink with others state that they talk and socialize when drinking. Relatively few, only 6 percent, listen to music or watch television when drinking with others. The diversity among the women is pronounced and points once again to the heterogeneity of alcoholic women.

Over one-half of the women drink with people from their neighborhood. In general, however, they drink less than usual when with neighbors, co-workers and family members. They tend to abstain when with people from their church, and are most likely to drink the same amount as usual only when with close friends. Almost two-thirds of the women have close friends whom they perceive as having a drinking problem, and 20 percent of these women believe these friendships have resulted in an increase in their own drinking. The findings reported here are remarkably similar to the national surveys that report up to 66 percent of the women interviewed know someone who drinks "too much" (Johnson et al., 1977, p. 23).

Drinking among friends and neighbors

We were also interested in determining the existence of heavy drinking among the women's friends and neighbors. Of particular interest was the prevalence of problem drinking among other women in the neighborhood.

Of the 117 study women who have some acquaintances in their neighborhood, almost two-thirds know women who drink heavily, with 30 percent stating that some of these other women have had treatment. Of those study women who know men with serious drinking problems, 24 percent of them have had help. These findings clearly indicate that there are substantial numbers of women and men who drink heavily and who have not had treatment. Yet the percentage of treated friends and neighbors seems to be high. While these other problem drinkers may indeed be "hidden" from the perspective of treatment agencies, they do not appear to be "hidden" from at least some of their heavy-drinking female neighbors.

In addition to providing a very rough estimate of the prevalence of alcoholism among friends and neighbors of alcoholic women, these data were also useful in examining social interactions and variations in drinking patterns. Twenty-two percent of the subjects do not know *anyone* in their neighborhood. Professional and unmarried employed women are least likely to know anyone in their neighborhood and may be the most isolated of the study women. They are also less likely to be exposed to neighbors who drink heavily. It is the unemployed women, independent of marital status, who are more likely to know heavy-drinking neighbors, and who, it will be recalled, are also more likely to drink with others rather than alone.

Secrecy in drinking

As mentioned earlier, the decision to study a suburban-urban population was based on certain premises about likely differences in life styles. One major area of interest is the openness, or alternately the secrecy, which the women from these two locales maintain about their drinking. It is here that the most unexpected findings emerged. From the start, secrecy was viewed as forming a continuum; it was thought (Hypothesis 1) that secret drinking was more likely to be found among suburban housewives and least likely among the professional women.

It was assumed that the suburban housewife, who has less opportunity for casual social contacts, would be more discreet because of the likely greater visibility of her behavior with friends and neighbors. In contrast, the professional woman was perceived as having many opportunities for more casual social contacts with a lessened degree of intimacy, and thus she would be seemingly more open about drinking.

The study women were specifically asked if they hid their drinking. At varying times almost three-fourths (73 percent) attempted to hide their drinking and somewhat more than a third (37 percent) were still hiding their drinking as they entered treatment. The locale in which the women lived, socioeconomic status, and the quantity the women usually drink all showed significant differences. As predicted, more of the suburban (84 percent) as compared to urban women (65 percent) said they hid their drinking ($p < .05$).

The professional women were just as likely to report hiding their drinking as the other women studied; there were, however, significant differences in support of the original study hypothesis if the professional women lived in an *urban* community. Fewer urban professional women hid their drinking when compared to suburban professional women and looked much like their urban nonprofessional counterparts on this variable. Though not a significant difference, more of the suburban professional women report hiding their drinking (91 percent) when compared to the other women ($p < .07$).

Consistent with the findings on solitary drinking, the higher the socioeconomic status of the woman, the more likely she is to hide her drinking ($p < .05$). Of the women in the highest and middle socioeconomic group, 83 and 78 percent, respectively, hid their drinking; in contrast, fewer, 61 percent, in the lowest socioeconomic group hid their drinking.

In addition, the usual amount of liquor consumed daily is related to whether or not the women hide their drinking. The greater the quantity of liquor consumed, the less likely is an attempt made to hide drinking ($p < .01$). While over 80 percent of the women who drink less than 11 drinks daily hide their drinking, only 53 percent of the very heavy drinkers do so.

Thus, there seems to be some support for the original study hypothesis, since differences were found by the woman's urban and suburban residence. But, rather than the suburban housewife being the most secretive and the professional woman the least secretive, the overriding variable is the suburban-urban residence of the women, with more of the suburban study women hiding their drinking than the urban women. In addition, the higher the socioeconomic status of the woman, the more likely she is to hide her drinking. The original hypothesis can be refined and restated: Secret drinking is more likely to be found among suburban women and those of high and middle socioeconomic status; secret drinking is least likely among urban and the lowest socioeconomic women, and it is not related to the woman's professional status, unless she lives in a suburban community. Secrecy in drinking seems more related to the woman having a current affiliation and financial security; this, in turn, may reinforce a perceived need for secrecy.

These findings on secrecy are consistent with those discussed earlier on solitary drinking and also support those of other studies designed to control the socioeconomic status of women alcoholics (Lisansky, 1957, 1958).

Social-escapist reasons for drinking

Further predictions were made about differences that might be found among the different groups of women and the reasons they would give for their drinking. It was thought that more of the professional women, because of their greater opportunity for interacting with others, would give more social reasons for drinking as compared to the other women, including other women who work (Hypothesis 2).

It was further assumed that women living in the suburbs, by contrast, would be more likely to have escapist reasons for drinking as compared to the other women studied (Hypothesis 3). This hypothesis was based on a perception of a more constricted life style for the suburban woman, more of whom would be tied to home, family, and children with less opportunity for satisfying interactions with others and therefore drinking as a means of escape.

A number of questions that are believed to reflect accurately social and escapist reasons for drinking were asked (Cahalan, Cisin, and Crossley, 1969). Four items constitute the social drinking scale and five are used in the escapist scale.[8] The only variable significantly related to social reasons for drinking was race. Black women in the study were much more likely to give a social reason for drinking than were white women in the study ($p < .01$). This finding on social reasons may be a clue to a different meaning given to alcohol in the black community and differences in drinking expectations (Harper 1976).

Based on five escapist reasons for drinking, the women studied had an average (mean) score of 4.1. Escapist reasons for drinking obviously best characterize all the women, and this is consistent with Knupfer's discussion (1963) of cross-pressures for women: If the norm is for women to drink moderately and she drinks heavily, then the woman is more likely to have escape reasons for drinking.

When the average scores are compared by the urban-suburban residence of the women, women living in the suburbs have a score of 4.29 while women living in an urban locale have a score of 4.0. This difference is not at the .05 significance level established for the study, although approaching it ($p < .14$).

When mean scores are compared by age, significant differences emerge. The woman who is still in her twenties is much more likely to give an escapist reason for drinking (4.6) than a woman in her forties (3.9) ($p < .05$).

Thus, while most study women tend to offer escapist rather than social reasons for drinking, black women are more likely to give social reasons, but they are equally likely to give an escapist reason when compared to white women; only younger women, those under age 30, are significantly more likely to offer an escapist reason for their drinking.

Drinking with other drug use

Accurate data on alcohol and other drug use is difficult to obtain. A review of the literature on conjoint alcohol and drug abuse indicates that approximately 20 percent of drug-dependent individuals use alcohol in conjunction with some other addicting drugs, and that conjoint use is more common among younger than it is among older people (Freed, 1973). Gender differences are striking; Curlee (1970) notes that 20 percent of the male and 43 percent of the female alcoholics used minor tranquilizers and sedatives, with 10 percent of the male and 25 percent of the female alcoholics dependent on other drugs. Rathod and Thompson (1971) reported similar findings; 20 percent of the male and 27 percent of the female alcoholics were dependent on amphetamines and barbiturates. Bremmer (1967) attributed the higher death rate for female alcoholics in accidents to conjoint alcohol and barbiturate use. Female alcoholics have a death rate 16 times the expected rate while the rate for male alcoholics is 6 times the expected rate.

The women in the present study were asked if they ever used a number of specific drugs. If they did, they were then asked how frequently they used a drug, if they used it in the last three months, if they drank when using it, and for how long they had used the drug.

Eighty-two percent of the subjects report having used other drugs in addition to alcohol at some time in their lives. While not always taken while drinking, the use of other depressants, especially tranquilizers and sleeping pills, by these women is particularly high. Eighty-seven percent of the women who have ever taken other drugs have used tranquilizers or sedatives, and almost two-thirds have used them within three months prior to the interview. When using tranquilizers, over one-half have taken them daily and one-half have used them for over one year.

The use of tranquilizers is followed closely by the use of sleeping pills and the use of stimulants; 52 percent and 26 percent respectively of all subjects who have ever used other drugs. Of particular interest is the finding that almost one-half of the subjects report that they have used other drugs *while drinking;* a majority report using more than one other drug on these occasions. As the case with drug use in general, the most frequently used drugs while drinking are tranquilizers (by 42 percent of all study women who ever used other drugs); sleeping pills (24 percent); stimulants (15 percent); and marijuana (14 percent).

Using a mean score of other drug usage, the amount of such drug taking while drinking varies by race, age, and the usual amount of alcohol consumed. White subjects use significantly more drugs (1.12) while drinking than black subjects, .34 ($p < .05$); and subjects under age 30 use significantly more drugs (1.93) while drinking than do subjects over age 40 ($p < .05$). In addition, very heavy drinkers, who usually drink more than 15 drinks, use significantly more drugs (1.76) while drinking than do moderately heavy drinkers, who usually consume 5 to 11 drinks (.75). Thus white women—those who drink very heavy amounts of alcohol and those under 30—seem to run a considerably higher risk than the other women of experiencing the lethal effects of taking alcohol and other drugs in combination.

In an attempt to better understand patterns of alcohol and other drug usage, a further analysis was done of the types of drugs used by the 72 study women who combine alcohol and other drugs. This was done by reconceptualizing into two distinct categories the types of drugs used by these women. The first category includes the 58 women who predominantly use depressants (tranquilizers and sleeping pills) and/or stimulants and/or other drugs (marijuana, analgesics, diuretics). With the exception of marijuana, all of the drugs in this category are legal and can be obtained over-the-counter or by prescription. The second category includes the 14 women who predominantly use opiates (opium, heroin, methadone, codeine), and/or cocaine, and/or hallucinogens while drinking.

When the women in these two drug categories are compared with the women who do not use other drugs while drinking, only one significant difference emerges. White study women are much more likely to use depressants and/or stimulants while drinking than are black study women ($p < .001$). White and black women in the study do not differ significantly in the use of opiates, cocaine, or hallucinogens, and relatively few study women use these drugs while drinking. It is clear, however, that the black study women are less likely than white women to use *any* other drug while drinking.

These findings on drug usage were compared with those of Mulford (1977). While fewer, 24 percent, of his female alcoholic subjects used other drugs regularly, 48 percent of the women in the present study use other drugs while drinking. Regular use of depressants was reported only by 20 percent of the women in Mulford's study, but by 39 percent of the women in the present study. The use of narcotics was also significantly less in Mulford's sample, totalling less than 1 percent. These differences may well reflect demographic differences between the two samples. Mulford, however, did find polydrug use to be much more common among women than men alcoholics.

The present findings can also be compared with those of a national sample of American adults, aged 18 to 74, who were interviewed by Parry (1971). He found that the incidence of psychotropic drug use among American women (63 percent) was 20 percentage points higher than among men and that most of the variance was accounted for the tranquilizer-sedative group of drugs. While 82 percent of the subjects in the present study have used a variety of other drugs, 71 percent have used tranquilizers or sedatives, findings consistent with Parry's conclusion that among American women high alcohol consumption is definitely related to high prevalence rates in the use of psychotropic drugs.

Maintenance of drinking

The process and etiology of any dependence remains little understood; it is known, however, that some alcoholics probably have both a physiological as well as a psychological dependency on alcohol. However, Murphree (1976) contends: "Among the older and more naive approaches to understanding alcohol problems is the idea that the person gets 'addicted' and then cannot remain abstinent" (p. 138). "I doubt that physical dependence in the classic pharmacologic sense is the reason why most people who drink alcohol continue to drink" (p. 142). The "classic pharmacologic sense" refers to both (1) increased tolerance, that is, requiring more alcohol for the same effect, and (2) demonstrable physical effects, such as hand tremors, if alcohol is withdrawn. Thus, Murphree, among others, does not believe physiological reasons account for the persistence of excessive drinking.

Recent research also does not support physiological reasons by themselves as accounting for the maintenance of heavy drinking. However, a variety of indicators used in this study demonstrate the likely presence of a physiological dependence for a considerable number of the women; for example, a great many (69 percent) admitted to their hands shaking in the morning after drinking and a similar proportion (63 percent) have had a drink first thing in the morning to "steady their nerves." An even larger number (84 percent) are aware that when they start drinking they cannot stop. Such responses could be viewed as pointing to the presence of a physical need for alcohol. Yet most of the women seem unaware of their own dependency on alcohol, although a large percentage recognize they have difficulty stopping once they start drinking. Relatively few (15 percent) make any statement that can be interpreted as awareness of a physiological or psychological dependency on alcohol. A considerable number (59 percent), however, do see themselves as having maintained their drinking for "the effect" of the alcohol (variously defined as to "forget," "relax," "feel better," "escape," "get high," and so on).

A slightly higher percentage (61 percent) believe they persist in their drinking because of their affective or feeling state such as being unhappy, lonely, anxious, or depressed. Significant relationships are found between the reasons for drinking, but in a sense these are negative relationships. Thus, of those *not* drinking because of their feeling state, they are significantly more likely to be drinking for the effect. Also, if a woman states she is maintaining her drinking because of a specific life situation she is significantly less likely to be drinking for the effect. When asked how much they would miss drinking if they gave it up entirely, 27 percent said they would miss it a lot, 34 percent would miss it some or a little, 30 percent would not miss it at all, and 9 percent were not sure how much they would miss it. As might be expected, the very heavy drinkers were most likely to state that they would miss drinking "a lot" if they gave it up entirely ($p < .01$).

Summary and conclusions

The study women first started drinking at an average age of 21. Problem drinking began at age 33, an average of 12 years after drinking started. Both these findings are consistent with other studies indicating that alcoholic women generally begin drinking somewhat later than alcoholic men, and the period elapsing between the first drink and problem drinking is not significantly different for alcoholic men and women when comparisons are made with other available data.

An average of 6 years elapses between the time problem drinking begins and the time the women seek treatment. Because there is no comparative data on men from the same treatment population, it is not known if this period is "telescoped" for women. It is, however, a great deal shorter than the period that elapses between social drinking and problem drinking.

The women are more likely to be daily than binge drinkers, and are likely to be drinking hard liquor rather than wine or beer. When they seek treatment, they are consuming an average of 11 drinks daily. Urban women and urban nonprofessional women are found to be the heaviest drinkers. In addition, because the majority have never had more to drink than in the week before entering treatment, it appears that they are seeking help at the height of their drinking.

Only about one-half (51 percent) of the women report that problem drinking was preceded by some specific life pressure or event and tends not to support other studies that associate problem drinking for women with a critical life situation. Once problem drinking begins, two major reasons emerge for the persistence of drinking: feelings such as being unhappy, lonely, anxious, or depressed; or feelings of the pleasurable escapist effects of alcohol. As they enter treatment, there is a relative lack of understanding of any dependency centered on alcohol, even though a majority have demonstrable signs of both physiological and psychological dependency.

While the great majority of the women most often drink in their own homes, employed women also drink fairly often in restaurants and bars. The white professional woman of the highest socioeconomic status is the most likely to drink in restaurants and bars. The majority of the study women who most usually drink alone are the married women and the single employed women. The higher the socioeconomic status of the woman, the more likely she is to drink alone. Consistent with this, married women and suburban professional women (women of the highest socioeconomic status) are most likely to hide their drinking. Thus, it is speculated that these women with attachments to others, either through marriage or employment, may have a greater investment in maintaining secrecy about their drinking.

Unemployed women, on the other hand, are more likely to know neighbors who drink heavily and to drink with others. The finding that over one-half of the subjects drink with people from their neighborhood is of considerable interest. Almost two-thirds of the women who have neighborhood acquaintances know heavy-drinking women, and 40 percent of these study women report that none of these women acquaintances have received help for their drinking problem. Even when interpreted conservatively—since many report knowing more than one other female heavy drinker—these findings are indicative of substantial numbers of heavy-drinking women, most likely unemployed, who are not receiving treatment.

It was thought (Hypothesis 1) that secret drinking would more likely be found among suburban housewives and least likely among professional women. However, the data show that secret drinking is more likely to be found among suburban women, but is independent of the women's professional status. It is related instead to having a current affiliation, either in work or marriage, and to having a higher socioeconomic status.

It was also thought (Hypothesis 2) that professional women would be more likely to give social reasons for drinking than the other women, including other employed women. However, the data show that professional women are less (although not significantly) likely to give social reasons for drinking than are nonprofessional women. It was also expected (Hypothesis 3) that women living in the suburbs would be more likely to be escapist drinkers than the other women studied. Yet, in fact, most women in the study offered escapist rather than social reasons for drinking. While suburban women are somewhat more likely to be escapist drinkers than urban women, the difference between the groups did not reach significance. Women under age 30 are most likely to give an escapist reason for drinking.

In addition to their problems with alcohol, the great majority of subjects have used other drugs at some time in their lives. Almost one-half of the women have used other drugs *while drinking*, with white subjects using more depressants and/or stimulants than black subjects. Relatively few women in this study have used opiates, cocaine, or hallucinogens, and the use of such drugs does not vary by race. Black women are less likely than white women to use *any* type of drug other than alcohol.

It is the white women, those under age 30, and the very heavy drinkers who are most likely to use other drugs while drinking. While it is not surprising that younger subjects use more drugs than older subjects and are more likely to give an escapist reason for drinking, it is alarming that the heaviest drinkers (those usually drinking more than 15 drinks daily) combine other drugs with alcohol. Obviously it is this group who run a very high risk of an overdose of alcohol and other drugs.

Several of these findings emerge as significant challenges to longstanding beliefs. The relatively short period between the onset of problem drinking and treatment casts doubt on the belief that most women who enter treatment have avoided it for prolonged periods. The drinking behavior of employed women, especially white professionals who cluster in the higher socioeconomic group, is probably as visible as that of men. Also, unemployed women, because they are more likely to know heavy-drinking neighbors and to drink with others, are quite visible.

The present study offers only partial support to the conclusion of Schuckit and Morrissey (1976): "Lower-status alcoholic women have drinking problems quite similar to those reported for the average alcoholic male, while higher status women more closely fit the stereotype in the literature of alcoholism among females" (p. 11).

One prevailing view explored is that alcoholic women are more likely than alcoholic men to hide their drinking and drink in their own home. Some studies (Lisansky, 1958; Cramer and Blacker, 1966) indicate, however, that this tends to be valid only for higher status alcoholic women. In the present study, socioeconomic status is positively related to marital and employment status, occupation as a professional, and race. It is the married woman of the highest socioeconomic status who is most likely to hide her drinking from others. Consistent with this, the married and employed woman of the highest socioeconomic status is most likely to drink alone. Thus, it seems to be true that married women of the highest socioeconomic status best exemplify the stereotype of alcoholic women hiding their drinking and drinking alone.

The findings of the present study on drinking in restaurants and bars do not, however, confirm those of Cramer and Blacker (1966), who found that lower-status women are more likely to be bar drinkers. While the women are most likely to drink in their own home, white employed professional women of the highest socioeconomic status drink fairly often in restaurants and bars. This may be a reflection of changing cultural norms, further reinforcing the notion that alcoholic women cannot be validly stereotyped. While married women of high socioeconomic status continue to conform to the stereotype of secret, solitary drinking, employed high-status women do not. Thus, it might be expected that as women's roles continue to change, the drinking patterns of women will also change.

Notes
1. Only six subjects started to drink before the age of 13 and the majority perceived themselves to be alcoholic before the age of 20.

2. Heavy drinkers are defined as those who drink nearly every day with five or more drinks at a sitting at least once in a while; or at least weekly with usually five or more drinks on most occasions, Cahalan, Cisin, and Crossley (1969). The Quantity-Frequency-Variability Index is discussed in some detail by Cahalan, Cisin, and Crossley (1969, pp. 212–215). Essentially the *type* of beverage most often drunk (beer, wine, or spirits), how *often* the person has five or six drinks (or three, or four, or one, or two drinks), and the most usual (modal) amount consumed and the highest amount drunk on occasion are considered. The arbitrary labels of the classification scheme are recognized and the difficulty of achieving agreement on "heavy" or "infrequent" noted. As a result the authors introduced a volume-variability index which they suggest is less complicated. The scale is based on: (1) the individual's average daily volume and (2) the division of several daily-volume groups into additional sub-groups according to how variable the person's drinking is from day to day.
3. Room notes that one-half pint is taken as the liquor equivalent of 6–7 drinks of any beverage; one pint, 12 drinks of any beverage (p. 15).
4. We were assisted in developing this measure by Don Cahalan and Robin Room. The latter suggested a procedure to cover amounts above five drinks, and this essentially is the method described.
5. Defined as heavy drinking at intervals and then little or moderate drinking in between these intervals of continuous drinking, which usually last more than a day (Keller and McCormick, 1968).
6. The definition of "heavier" is considerably less than specified in note 2.
7. This is not too dissimilar from national survey data suggesting consistency among women; 38 percent of female drinkers with problems are reported to drink "sometimes or often" when doing chores (Johnson et al., 1977, p. 58).
8. *Social reasons:* "to be sociable," "people I know drink," "to celebrate special occasions," "to be polite." *Escapist reasons:* "to relax," "to forget everything," "to forget worries," "to cheer up," "I need when nervous."

4
Consequences of Drinking

Summary of findings
Suburban women are more likely to be criticized about their drinking than urban women.

Continuous heavy drinking for more than one day is frequent for many of the women; more of the urban women (60 percent) than suburban women (36 percent) report they are frequently likely to be high for more than one day.

Some 84 percent of the women who enter treatment for their drinking problems perceive women to be rejected more than men for being problem drinkers.

Almost half of the women changed their social lives to accommodate their heavy drinking.

Many women find drinking interferes with their sexual relations. A smaller proportion of women report heightened sexual interest because of their drinking, and these women are significantly more likely to report an increase in their sexual satisfaction.

Most of the women (77 percent) concur that others believe women are more sexually available when they are drinking than when they are not drinking. A majority of the women did not describe their drinking as influencing their sexual behavior.

Almost half of the women experienced injuries as a result of heavy drinking: Falling and burns were a frequent occurrence, and for many hospitalization was necessary.

When women enter treatment for alcoholism, they show a high degree of psychophysiological symptoms, in addition to their alcoholism.

Psychological and physiological dependency is often not recognized by the women. For example, tremors and an increase in tolerance, needing more alcohol to achieve the same effect, are not put within the context of a physiological dependency.

Those women found to be very heavy drinkers (over 15 drinks) were most likely to have the highest average (mean) score reflecting interference in a number of aspects of their life: family, social life, job, and health.

I woke this morning to a sunny day in a Key West, Florida, campground. I heard the report of a camper's death across the narrow canal. The police car was still there. The motor home was from New Jersey. A coincidence. At first most of us assumed that an older man died. The details differed. It was a woman of 30, dead of an overdose of alcohol combined with other drugs. She drank heavily, said her relatives, and also took pills, which she told them were harmless.

In this chapter no attempt is made to deal with death per se as a consequence of heavy drinking (Haberman and Baden, 1978). The women about whom we are writing were obviously not well when first interviewed for the study, and they were already experiencing in varying degrees some of the severe consequences of their alcoholic drinking.

The data presented here were elicited to capture some of the major areas in which consequences can be measured, areas that speak at the same time about the diversity of a woman's life affected by alcohol. Little research has been available concerning the consequences of drinking for alcoholic women. One recent exception reports on recent national surveys (Johnson et al., 1977). Measures used to assess such consequences have been derived from those developed for male alcoholics and cannot be applied directly with any degree of validity to a population whose socialization, development, and life tasks are so dissimilar. The consequences of drinking for men, as an example, have often been measured in relation to troubles with the police or on the job, areas that are likely to reflect negative consequences for more men than women in any comparison made because of the greater likelihood of the male being in the work place, engaging in public drinking, and "acting out" the consequences of drinking by driving while intoxicated or becoming belligerent in a public setting. In contrast, women, though part of the work force in increasing numbers, are not always in the labor force, and thus their drinking behavior and the consequences for them may be quite different and less visible, except possibly to family and friends who are aware of a drinking problem. Others around the women, however, may believe still that cigarette burns, and frequent falls may just be carelessness, not due instead to their drinking.

The social stigma associated with drinking by women is discussed first in this chapter. An area relatively lacking in data is also given attention: the sexual response and interest of alcoholic women in sex, their view of the sexual behavior of drinking women, their own behavior, and finally the relationship between their own interest and the satisfaction they experience.

As has often been done in research on alcoholism, the specific troubles experienced as a result of drinking are assessed. An expanded list of possible "troubles," seemingly more appropriate to women, are used here. The emotional health of the women as they began treatment was examined using a standardized measure that could be repeated at the time of the follow-up. Finally, four specific scales were developed for this study to measure more precisely the effect of drinking on family, social life, work, and physical health.

The findings should facilitate the work of therapists in understanding some of the possible extensive consequences of women's drinking. It should also foster an interest in examining more critically some of the assumptions about drinking women. Finally, it may spur other researchers to explore in greater detail areas not examined in depth in the present study.

Stigma reinforcement

Clearly, there is a complex background of norms and mores surrounding a woman who drinks. The belief has developed that heavy drinking for a woman is not "ladylike" and is more heavily stigmatized than it is for a man. Thus, while the label of being an alcoholic falls very heavily on both women and men, it is perceived as worse for a woman to be an alcoholic. At the time this study was conducted societal norms still imposed different codes of behavior—and more rigid ones—for women than for men. Women, for example, do not, as a rule, do their drinking in bars. Thus, while it probably is acceptable and comfortable for women to do their drinking in bars in some communities, more likely this is a neighborhood bar where there is a strong feeling of cohesiveness; or a transient bar (such as a singles bar); or a cocktail lounge; or on the road—at airports, or in railroad or bus stations; or at a "lunch" bar, the kind that abound in business districts. The bar trade is still predominantly male, and although this may change rapidly in the coming years as more women enter diverse occupations, there are certain bars into which women do not enter easily, or at all. Thus, open casual drinking by women in public places is not part of the societal expectation of our time, except as part of the ritual of a meal, or of some socially approved group. Women drinking alone in a bar is still taboo. The woman who does not adhere to these expectations may be viewed as promiscuous, as possibly alcoholic, and certainly as deviant from the norm.

Data from recent national surveys indicate that 42 percent of the males report some drinking at bars; in contrast, only 23 percent of the females report such behavior. This is, of course, not necessarily drinking alone (Johnson et al., 1977, p. 59).

The study women were asked: "Does anyone criticize you because of your drinking?" Those who answered in the affirmative were then asked: "Who did the criticizing?" All but 16 percent acknowledged negative comments, and they most usually experienced criticism by more than one person, on the average 1.6. The only background variables for which differences are found are place of residence, religious background, and the treatment setting from which the women were selected. Suburban women are likely to experience criticism by significantly more persons than urban women. In fact, the urban women are three times as likely (24 percent) as the suburban women (8 percent) to report having escaped criticism. The suburban women's greater likelihood of being criticized may fit with the greater visibility of their drinking in a family setting than is true for the urban women in this study group, who are less likely to be married.

Catholic women, as compared with Protestant women combined with other religious affiliations, experience greater criticism. Obviously, criticism most often comes from family members and friends who may be from similar religious backgrounds to the women. If this is the case, it is possible that Catholics experience more ambivalence about drinking for women, and possibly men, too, than do Protestants.

Cahalan, Cisin, and Crossley's (1969) study of American drinking practices call attention to Catholic men having the highest proportion of heavy drinkers among men of any religious group. In Cahalan and Room's later work (1974) in which they report the extension of their research to a study of American men who are problem drinkers, the interaction between ethnicity and religion is also noted. In more recent national surveys, Catholics have the highest percentage of problem drinkers for both men and women; it is noted, too, that Catholics are more often drinkers (Johnson et al., 1977, p. 56).

The treatment settings from which the women were selected show differences in the average number of persons criticizing a woman for her drinking. The AA women were found to have fewer persons criticizing them, on the average, while those who are inpatients report significantly more persons being critical. The fact that women inpatients experience criticism by more persons in their lives can probably be best understood in the context of their drinking likely being more evident to others prior to treatment than either the women who were selected from outpatient clinics or from AA groups.

Criticism by others is seen as reinforcing a view already held by most women, namely, that their drinking is under their own control. This perception does not take account of the process of the psychological or physiological dependency that may have occurred. Alcohol is a mood-altering drug; this is one of the reasons small quantities are at first found to offer relief from anxiety. Since it alters perception as well as mood, it is often used initially to lessen the impact of life's stresses and expectations. As more and more alcohol is required to achieve the same effect, an increase in tolerance occurs, and the process of physiological dependency begins. For example, morning drinking after some sleep obviously follows a period of several hours without alcohol. The withdrawal process from alcohol, which occurs during sleep, sets in motion a physiological need for alcohol. Early on in drinking, there may be a slight tremulousness following withdrawal of alcohol, but later on, hands will be very unsteady, and there may even be great difficulty in holding a drink or any object. Thus, a physiological and/or psychological need for alcohol may be present but not recognized by the person drinking.

Most organized religions and individuals, however, stress individual culpability rather than the development of a process of dependency. Until those who drink persistently, their families and close associates perceive that heavy drinking results in a dependency process, as with any drug, then self-criticism as well as criticism by others will persist. The circular process of heavy drinking leading to *needing* to drink to ward off painful symptoms of either physiological or psychological withdrawal is not fully understood. The interactions of women, however, with the significant others in their lives, including organized religion and professional helpers, often reinforce a belief that heavy drinking is under the drinkers' control.

High for more than one day

Physiologically, a state of unconsciousness often intervenes when the amount of alcohol exceeds certain limits, as happens with any nervous system depressant. Nonetheless, an assessment was made of the extensiveness of each woman's drinking. We asked if she ever became intoxicated for a period of time exceeding more than the current day in which she began her drinking. This occurred in varying degrees of frequency for almost three-fourths of the women (72 percent). As few as 20 percent of the women stated this had never happened during their periods of heavy drinking. An additional 8 percent gave no information on this question. For 14 percent, it was four or fewer occasions, an additional 8 percent had between five to nine occurrences, with most of the women, 50 percent, reporting frequent occasions (10 or more) of being high for more than one day.

There is no significant variation by the background variables except in relation to their urban-suburban residence: Sixty percent of the urban women were frequently (10 or more times) likely to be high for more than one day as compared to 36 percent of the suburban women. This particular finding may reflect differences in the social controls that operate in suburban areas for women and that do not exist in urban communities. However, such a pattern of continuous "highs" for the urban women seems to indicate a lessened capacity for functioning in other life spheres such as work.

Perceived social rejection for problem drinking

Asking the women a series of questions about how they think women problem drinkers are perceived by others, as compared with men, obviously tells something about how they perceive themselves. When asked if they thought women are rejected more socially because of their drinking than men are, the women overwhelmingly responded in the affirmative: Some 84 percent of the women thought women more rejected than men. And there is no variation in their responses by the major background variables.

Next, we asked a value-laden question: "Is it worse for a man or worse for a woman to drink too much, or is there no difference?" Only 5 percent of the women thought it is worse for a man, with 44 percent thinking it worse for a woman, and 51 percent believing there is no difference. To our surprise, significantly more of the suburban women (61 percent) as compared to the urban women (40 percent) thought there is no difference. Only one other background variable showed a significant difference. More of those not currently married but employed (63 percent) thought it worse for a woman to drink too much. This is one of the subgroups of women who are most likely to hide their drinking. They may be more isolated socially, too, because of their marital status, and interact less with others who are aware of the extent of their drinking.

Finally, the women were asked if, because of their drinking, they themselves are rejected in some way, who does the rejecting, and what form it takes. Friends and husbands were most often mentioned by 53 percent of the women but almost as many (47 percent) said they experience no rejection. Generally, when rejection was acknowledged by a study woman, she said it involved knowing that others do not want to associate with her. Many of the women seemed reluctant to acknowledge having experienced rejection and seemed to have difficulty in stating *how* they are rejected. Because this question was not very productive, it could be viewed as indicating the painfulness of this particular area. Next, we explored the impact of drinking on the women's social life.

Social life

When there is concern about revealing yourself, one classic avoidance technique is to decrease social ties. As a result of drinking, almost half of the women say they have changed friends or isolated themselves from a variety of their usual social activities. Even more of the suburban women describe this behavior as a result of their drinking than do the urban women. If the suburban women have a more active social life to begin with, the difference between suburban and urban women may not be as great as it appears. Nonetheless, the women in the suburbs are more likely to describe decreasing social contacts as well as leaving the house less frequently. Clearly, their social life changes to accommodate their drinking. This particular behavior on the part of the women can best be understood when placed in the context of their awareness of how others perceive their drinking problem as well as their own self-perceptions.

In some measure, the women seem to compensate for this loss of old friends and activities by substituting other friends and activities that fit more agreeably with their heavy drinking behavior. Slightly more than a third (35 percent) of the women describe acquiring new contacts because of their drinking; this involves either people whom they meet in bars or neighbors. Co-workers account for relatively few new friends (3 percent).

To better discriminate among the various subgroups of women and the effect of drinking on their social life, a number of the indicators used to assess social activity were combined to form an isolation index. This isolation index is based on six items. Three questions concern the degree of isolation, two focus on the extent of social activities, and one question concerns leaving the house. The questions requiring a yes or no response are:

1. I am beginning to cut myself off from old friends because of my drinking.
2. I go out of the house, but I see a limited number of people because of my drinking.

3. I engage in a few social activities, only what is necessary.
4. I have cut myself off from friends.
5. I often do not leave the house, except to buy liquor.
6. I do not engage in any social activities.

About one-sixth did not report the presence of any item indicating social isolation. In contrast, just one-fourth scored at the extreme end of the scale, responding positively to five or six items. The higher the score, the greater the isolation. The average (mean) score for all the women is 2.85, with a standard deviation of 2.05. When this index is related to the various background variables, including the quantity the woman usually drinks, only age emerges as a significant variable, with those under 40 years being the most isolated. It may be recalled that age is related to marital status with the younger women less likely to be married. It is probably true that without marriage there is greater isolation for many of the women. This is an area that other researchers may wish to pursue to understand better such isolation and its effect.

TABLE 4-1 *Isolation Index: Percentage Distribution*

SCALE SCORE	(N=150)
0–1	35
2–4	40
5–6	25

Sexual behavior of alcoholic women

The sensitivity of others concerning a woman's sexual response while drinking may well account for this lack of data. Yet until we have such data there tends to be an exaggerated and probably inaccurate perception of the relationship between alcohol and a woman's sexual behavior.

It is known that with the drinking of alcoholic beverages there is a lessening of inhibitions. This again can be related to alcohol acting as a depressant on the central nervous system. Higher levels of alcohol in the blood also impair cognitive functioning. Because alcohol so clearly interferes with a person's judgment, this aspect is especially im-

Consequences of Drinking 69

portant as it relates to the effects of alcohol on behavior. As a result, women are often perceived as vulnerable to sexual experiences while they are drinking. A further reason for viewing them as vulnerable may be that for alcoholic women a sexual experience indicates acceptance, something that may be missing from their current life.

We explored with the study respondents their perceptions of heavy-drinking women and sexual behavior. They were subsequently asked to describe the effect of drinking on their own sexual behavior. Initially we asked: "Do you think people believe women are more sexually available when they are drinking than when they are not drinking?" The women were almost unanimous; 77 percent said this was the most common view.

We also asked if one consequence of their drinking has been their own sexual involvement with someone they would not have been involved with otherwise. Slightly more than two-fifths of the women (43 percent) did acknowledge this as a consequence of their drinking. In addition, a relatively small percentage (27 percent) believe they were taken advantage of sexually at some time. These women say that when this did occur, it is likely to have happened on more than one occasion. A similar pattern is described by women who report having sexual experiences with someone whom they would not have otherwise. And for only one-fifth was it limited to a single occasion. It thus appears that when a woman who drinks heavily becomes sexually involved as a consequence of her drinking, she is most likely to have this involvement on more than one occasion and not necessarily with the same person.

Yet the support for women's sexual vulnerability seems mixed and even weak. Most women do not believe they are sexually used because of their drinking, but at the same time many describe sexual liaisons that would not have otherwise occurred had they not been drinking heavily. Thus, one can infer that the women recognize their own responsibility, that is, some women acknowledge their drinking results in behavior in the area of sex that would not occur ordinarily.

For those women who had sexual relations connected with their drinking, the next question raised is whether this is more likely to occur for one subgroup of women rather than another. No differences are found by religion, socioeconomic status, or by the type of treatment setting. For all the other characteristics analyzed throughout this study significant differences are found. Thus, differences are seen by the women's professional status, race, marital status, the locale in which they live, marital and employment status, the quantity of drinks, and age. Women in the professions, white women, the divorced and the never married, the urban women, those not living with a spouse but employed, and those under 30 are all more likely to have such sexual involvement; for women over 40, there is a dramatically decreasing likelihood. Also, the larger the quantity the woman drinks, the increased likelihood there is of such an occurrence being reported; 61 percent of the very heavy drinkers (more than 15 drinks) as compared to 16 percent of the low-heavy drinkers (those who drink less than 5 drinks) attribute such sexual liaisons to their drinking.

Thus, the women who do not have the constraints of marriage or possibly have more opportunities and options by living in an urban area, are younger, better educated (the professional women), drink very heavily, or are employed are most likely to have sexual involvements as a result of drinking.

Those study women who report no sexual experiences which they connect with drinking—*and this is true for a majority of the study women*—are significantly more likely to believe that women who drink are *not* more available sexually while drinking. Conversely, women who acknowledge being more available to sexual experience while drinking perceive this to be true for all women. It seems, then, that perceptions and behavior are closely related in this particular area, that is, the perception of the sexual activity of women who drink heavily is influenced by their own experiences.

As to their sexual orientation, almost all of the women indicated their preference is for a man as sexual partner. Only nine women (6 percent) of the study group state their sexual interest is primarily in another woman. Since this figure is somewhat less than estimates given for the general population, it can be viewed as a conservative response.

Drinking, it was thought, would interfere with the sexual relations of some women while increasing the interest, and possibly the sexual satisfaction, of others. A sizable number of women (33 percent) said their sex drive increases after drinking. Since it was thought that this increased interest in sex may characterize the same group of women who stated that drinking also increases their sexual satisfaction, this possibility, too, was explored. Those women who report greater sexual interest because of their drinking are significantly more likely to indicate an increase in their sexual satisfaction (59 percent) as compared to those (12 percent) who report increased satisfaction without an increase in interest ($p < .001$). Thus, there seems to be support for the belief that alcohol—and, no doubt, other mind-altering drugs—enhance the sexual satisfaction of some women who are not ordinarily able to gain satisfaction. Most likely, when the sexual freedom enjoyed by increasing numbers of women permeates the American culture, the previous burden for some women in sexual relationships will be altered, and satisfaction may be possible for more women, without alcohol. Yet limited sexual satisfaction without alcohol cannot be viewed as a cause of women's alcoholism. Rather, increased satisfaction most obviously becomes a side effect of heavy drinking for those women who then become more free to enjoy their sexuality.

In contrast to these women, a larger number (46 percent) said drinking interfered with their sexual relations. The most common interference cited was a loss of interest on their part; relatively few women (4.3 percent) said their partners refused sex with them while they were drinking. How accurate this is may be questioned by some and seems challenged by the husband interviews. Yet it remains the women's perception. It may well be, too, that relatively few have permanent attachments at this time.

Beyond the sexual area, a wide range of problems exist for alcoholic women, and we used a wide range of research techniques to attempt to capture these difficulties.

Problems as defined by the women

Since alcoholism is often defined in relation to its consequences, it seemed a necessary first step in thinking about women alcoholics to spell out in detail the consequences of their drinking. Very early in the interview the women were asked: "In what way has drinking presented problems for you?" This approach allowed the women to describe their problems prior to introducing a checklist. All of the spontaneously described problems had been anticipated in the checklist of problems subsequently presented to the women.

The women's responses to the more open general question on problems were classified into 17 specific problems. Most frequently cited was fear of being unable to carry out their job, including the fear of losing it. This may be a somewhat surprising finding for those who view women with a drinking problem as persons confined to their homes. Closer to this traditional perception of the women is the problem cited next most frequently by the study women, namely, difficulty in functioning as mothers.

Almost three-fourths of the women mentioned two or more problems, an average of 2.3. Their general functioning, job performances, their role as mothers, and blackouts were among the four major problem areas spontaneously attributed to drinking. There is no significant variation in the average number of problems elicited by this open-ended approach by any of the major background variables, except for socioeconomic status. Women in the higher socioeconomic subgroup have the highest average number of problems. Yet this is viewed as likely to be a spurious finding because those with more education are usually more articulate and thus responses to open-ended questions tend to be inflated for them, and this is especially apparent when quantified as was done here.

Troubles resulting from drinking

Traditionally, research in alcoholism has applied the concept of "troubles" as a result of drinking.[1] The number of questions used in such a trouble score have varied oftentimes from study to study (Cahalan et al., 1969, Edwards et al., 1972, Corrigan, 1974a), but essentially Mulford's early work (1960) in this field has been the basis for such an approach. A fairly consistent finding is that of Edwards and associates, among others, who report women have fewer troubles due to drinking than men. Yet he found that women who drink the same quantity as men experience no difference in the mean number of troubles.

One major interest of the present study is in determining the social and psychological consequences of drinking for women. Thus, a large number of questions not included in prior research are asked in the present study. Yet to allow for comparisons with previous studies, many of those same items that are usually included in a trouble-score inventory are discussed. The specific items discussed in this section are shown in Table 4–2. The first thirteen items in the table are traditionally included in studies where such "troubles" are described. Items

TABLE 4-2 *Troubles Resulting from Drinking (in percent)*

ITEM	POSITIVE RESPONSES (N=150)
1. Have you ever spent more money than you ought to on drink?	78
2. Have you ever gone without drink for a period to prove you can do so?	72
3. Have you ever had financial problems due to drinking?	40
4. Have you ever been in trouble with the police due to a "drunk" offense (other than drunk driving)?	14
5. Have you ever been in trouble with the police for drunk driving?	14
6. Have you ever been in trouble with the police for anything else connected with drinking?	15
7. Have you ever been in a road accident (as a driver or pedestrian) because of drinking?	21
8. Have you ever been in other accidents (for example, at home or at work) because of drinking?	42
9. After drinking, have you ever found you can't remember the night before? ("blackouts")	79
10. Do you ever find that when you start drinking you can't stop?	84
11. After drinking, have you found your hands shaky in the morning?	70
12. Have you ever had a drink first thing in the morning to steady your nerves or get rid of a hangover?	63
13. Have you ever "heard" or "seen" things due to drinking?	40
14. Attempted suicide?	27
15. Not able to cook, fairly often?	23
16. Not able to care for self, fairly often?	25
17. Not able to shop for food, fairly often?	22
18. Not able to care for home, fairly often?	33
Trouble Score Average (Mean) 7.59	
Standard Deviation 3.25	

14 through 18 have not been used previously in other trouble scores, but they seemed most germane, especially for a female population.

The high percentage of women who responded positively to most of the items is quite consistent with an alcoholic population. The number of accidents experienced by the women is quite high, both road accidents and those at home or work. The number of women who had trouble with the police is higher than expected, especially based on previous reports.

When an unduplicated count was obtained of the number of the women who had contacts with the police on offenses related to their drinking, it was found that 28 percent of the study group report this experience. Also, once in trouble with the police, many of the study women were likely to experience such trouble on more than one occasion. One woman reported that she was arrested for wrecking two cars while drinking and driving. Another said she was not charged by the police but was hospitalized, and on another occasion she was told by the police to pay the fare due a cabdriver, which she was stubbornly refusing to do. Still another became involved in disturbing the peace and assaulting a police officer. One woman was herself hit by a car while drinking, and still another was picked up for driving at what she recalls was 150 mph. She observed that she was afraid of killing herself or others.

The range of incidents involving women with the police seems to be quite similar to that of men. What seems lacking are only morals or sex offenses. The women were not asked if they had been arrested, or were they asked about the specifics of the charges made or about the disposition of any case. Here is an area that might well be given more systematic study.

The percentage of women reporting blackouts, inability to stop drinking once they start, tremors, morning drinking, and auditory or visual hallucinations is consistently quite high. As with other alcoholic populations, the number reporting an attempted suicide (27 percent) is beyond that found in the general population. Interference in traditional female tasks, such as shopping for food and cooking, elicit a positive response from a relatively small percentage of the women (less than 25 percent).

The average number of troubles is shown at the bottom of the table. Such a high trouble score of 7.59 with a standard deviation of 3.25 is consistent with the extent of troubles one would expect from a population of problem drinkers, but it is beyond what has been reported in other studies of women.

Cahalan and Room (1974) report on a general community population, including women, and thus the number identified with various problems is relatively low. Mulford's more recent report on women and men (1977) in treatment for drinking reviews ten troubles with an average of 2.5 troubles for female first admissions for treatment, as compared to a male mean trouble score of 3.2.

The average trouble score in this study was examined in relation to the ten background variables. Three variables show a statistically significant relationship: race, age and the quantity a woman drinks—but not socioeconomic status. White women, those under 40 years of age, and women who drink very heavily have a higher than average trouble score. This will be discussed further after the other measures describing the consequences of drinking have been presented.

Based on the national surveys cited earlier (Johnson, et al., 1977, p. 43), many of the "troubles" discussed here are described by those authors as "serious symptoms," and comparisons are made between women and men who are characterized as heavier drinkers. Most of these symptoms apply to 30 percent or substantially fewer of the heavier drinkers in the national surveys.[2] Some of the other "troubles" presented here are listed as "consequences" of drinking by Johnson and associates and are reported for between 4 percent and 6 percent of the women, including family complaints about spending too much on alcohol. Obviously the distinction between women designated heavy drinkers in national surveys and the alcoholic women in this study is most marked in the response to these questions, and the difference in results is most easily explained by the relatively low and different level of consumption of alcohol used in these national surveys to define the category "heavier drinkers."

Emotional health

The emotional health of alcoholic women is an area of great interest. There tends to be little in the way of firm data but much speculation. The speculation relates to the degree of "sickness" present in alcoholic women and the implications this has for their prognosis; also alcoholism as the primary diagnosis in contrast to alcoholism superimposed on an affective disorder, such as depression, is viewed as having a different course and outcome (Greenblatt and Schuckit, 1976). No such differential diagnosis was made for the study women, but some of the data that follow may be useful in this dialogue.

The women's emotional status was measured in the present study by applying the Twenty-Two Item Screening Score (Langner, 1962), which has been found to correlate with what psychiatrists judge to be psychiatric disorder, primarily psychoneurosis. The questions emphasize primarily psychophysiological symptoms such as shortness of breath, fainting spells, weakness, and so on. These symptoms have been found to be especially sensitive indicators of the emotional status of women (Bailey, 1967). A measure such as this is thought to be useful also in assessing changes from the initial interview to the follow-up interview one year later.

A score of four or more is frequently used to indicate psychiatric impairment; it also picks up some false-positives (Langner, 1962). Since some 90 percent of the women in the present study had this score, relatively few are free of symptoms. Using the more conservative score of 7 or more assures fewer errors in the assessment; 69 percent of the women had this higher score. One comparison group that has some relevance is Bailey's report (1967) on the *wives* of alcoholics, 74 percent of whom had 4 or more symptoms while their husbands were still drinking. In this same study, wives whose husbands have been sober for 6 months or more were less likely (44 percent) to have this score.

The average score at the time of the initial interview for the study women was 9.4. Within the background variables used for the study, almost every subgroup had a score of 7 or more. There is only one exception (married, employed women), which possibly can be attributed to the smaller size of this subsample. However, statistically significant differences are found in the emotional health impairment score by the women's occupational status (professional or nonprofessional), marital and employment status, age, and socioeconomic status. Such statistically significant differences, as we will explain later, are less important when there is a clear cutting point to indicate psychiatric impairment.

The professional women show significantly less impairment, scale score 8, than the women who are not in this category, scale score 10. As we have just noted, the women who are married and employed have significantly lower impairment (scale score 6) on this measure than those not married who are unemployed (scale score 11). Because of the relatively small number of women in this group, such a finding may well be due to sampling variation. The women between 30 and 39 years of age show the greatest impairment (scale score 11) when compared to those 40 or over (scale score 8). The highest socioeco-

Consequences of Drinking 77

nomic group are least impaired (scale score 8), while women in the lowest socioeconomic category have a significantly higher score (scale score 10). Women who drink the greatest quantity of alcohol, 15 or more drinks daily, also have a significantly higher average score (12.4), exceeding all other categories of the usual quantity of drinks consumed. No significant differences are found by the woman's marital status, race, or religion. Difference by the area of residence finds urban women with a scale score of 10 in contrast to the suburban women with a score of 9. This difference approaches significance ($p < .10$). The type of treatment setting at which the women are seen also reflect no significant differences.

It would be well to keep in mind that almost without exception these scores do reflect psychiatric impairment; however, the average score in each category does indicate whether there is a greater or lesser degree of impairment. The extensivenes of symptomatology is reflected in 37 percent of the women reporting 10 or more symptoms with 17 percent having as many as 15 of the 22 symptoms. The reason for the presence of so many symptoms is not clear. For example, does heavier drinking tend to exacerbate psychophysiological symptoms as measured here? Or does such symptomatology already exist and thus predate heavier drinking?

The data from the one year follow-up may give a better understanding of the relationship between these symptoms and heavy drinking. At the beginning of the study, it was thought that if women drank less one year later, there would be a decrease in such symptomatology. If such a decrease did occur, the quantity a woman drinks could plausibly be assumed to affect such symptomatology. If no such decrease in symptomatology did occur, then consideration could be given to the symptoms themselves as contributing to the heavy drinking, and a more serious underlying psychopathology would need to be considered. Yet, any decrease in symptomatology probably might not be expected to be directly proportional to any decrease in drinking within the year's time elapsing from the first interview, since this might be viewed as too brief a time span to bring about this change. If a substantial decrease in symptoms occurred with the alteration of drinking, then there would be support for giving primary attention to the cessation of drinking prior to attempting any form of psychotherapy for the myriad complaints a woman presents as she enters treatment. As discussed in detail in the chapter on the outcome of treatment, psychophysiological symptoms decrease as drinking decreases. Some researchers may wish, of course, to examine the direction of the cause-effect relationship and to consider whether or not a decrease of symptoms leads to a decrease in drinking. (We examine this perspective of causality in the chapter on treatment.)

Finally, we come to a description of the women's self-assessment of drinking and its effects.

Interference arising from drinking: Family, social, job, and health areas

Almost at the end of the interview, each woman was asked to complete a booklet containing 52 questions about how drinking affects her functioning. These questions were organized into four major areas: family relations, social relations, job functioning, and health. Each section of the booklet contained a minimum of 12 questions (social relations) and up to 14 questions (job functioning). The questions were introduced by asking the women if drinking interferes with any of these areas of their life. They were then asked if any of a number of specified experiences occurred.

An overview of the kind of questions posed in each section follows:

Family relations (a total of 12 questions): Frequent quarrels with family due to drinking? Husband left or asked me to leave because of drinking? My family has asked me to stop or reduce my drinking? . . .

Social relations (a total of 12 questions): Have few friends because of drinking? Have changed friends because of drinking? Do not leave the house, except to buy liquor? . . . (This section was the basis for the development of the isolation index discussed earlier.)

Job functioning (a total of 14 questions; asked only of women who ever worked in paid employment): Have had drinks during the work day on the job? Unemployed at present because of drinking? Intoxicated during the day at work? . . .

Health (a total of 13 questions): Have difficulty sleeping? Have injured self from falling or burning? Have been hospitalized because of drinking? . . .

At the end of the four sections just described, each woman rated the overall degree of interference on a scale of 1 to 4 with "1" indicating "no interference" and "4" reflecting "severe interference." These ratings were not used with anchoring descriptions but followed instead the series of questions which denoted problems in each specific area. The ratings are the women's self-perceptions. In Table 4–3 the mean score on the questions in each area and the self-ratings on degree of overall interference are presented. Congruence between the two measures is very high. As the mean scores increase, the severity of the self-rating of interference increases. The table also indicates significant differences found between the mean scores ($p < .001$). The largest number of women, about half, rate themselves as moderately to severely affected in two areas: family relations and health. Somewhat fewer, over one-third to two-fifths, see such an effect in job functioning and their social relations, respectively.

There is a relatively high proportion of women in every area who describe no interference but whose average score on the items relating to that area denotes the presence of some problems. For example, in the "health" area even women who report no interference have an average score of 4.0. Thus, it takes a relatively high average number of problems for these women to view themselves as having interference

TABLE 4–3 *Effects of Drinking[a]: Average (Mean) Score on Interference in Family, Social, Job, and Health Areas by Self-Rating of Degree of Interference*

AREAS RATED	SELF-RATING OF DEGREE OF INTERFERENCE IN AREA AND MEAN SCORE					
	Total[b]	*None*	*Mild*	*Moderate*	*Severe*	*P*
Family relations	(4.5) N=146	1.6 (N=27)	4.0 (N=44)	5.7 (N=44)	6.4 (N=31)	<.001
Social relations	(5.6) N=149	3.8 (N=34)	5.6 (N=56)	6.3 (N=32)	8.0 (N=27)	<.001
Job functioning	(4.1) N=126	2.0 (N=45)	3.7 (N=36)	5.9 (N=23)	7.3 (N=22)	<.001
Health	(6.5) N=146	4.0 (N=22)	5.7 (N=44)	7.1 (N=51)	9.0 (N=29)	<.001

[a] Except for health and family relations, which contained the same number of items (13), the scores can only be compared in absolute terms within each area and not across areas, since a slightly varied number of items were included (social, 12; job, 14). The higher the score the greater the interference.
[b] Omits "no answers"; job functioning is based only on the responses of those women who ever worked.

from drinking in their health or social relations. Family relations and job functioning may be more sensitive areas for the women since consistently lower scores are found for those reporting interference in contrast to social and health interference.

Since it is possible for some women to have entered treatment without perceiving interference in any area, this possibility was examined. Only one woman indicates "no interference" in any of the four areas, while eighteen others rate themselves as having at least mild interference. The one woman describing herself as having no interference actually responded positively to many of the questions reflecting problems in the family, job, and health areas. Her explanation for this final rating was that she was a member of AA for 3 months and had already experienced benefits in every one of these areas. In a sense, she was talking about the recovery process and we missed, in the self-rating only, the effects of drinking on this particular woman. This could well be interpreted as an interviewing failure and did not occur for the other women interviewed from AA.

Some 43 percent of the women describe mild, moderate, or severe interference owing to drinking in at least one of these areas. This also "fits" clinical impressions that those entering treatment are already experiencing difficulty in a number of critical areas of their lives.

Accessibility to intervention by professional helpers or AA should be high at this point. The specific areas of interference would need to be identified and could be the basis of early focused interventive efforts to engage a woman adequately in altering her drinking since so many of the study women are acutely aware of the effect on so many areas of their lives. Such an approach could possibly reduce the high early attrition from treatment.

Correlations between self-ratings of family, social, job, and health problems

A correlation matrix of the four self-ratings was carried out. The correlations were all relatively low, and little variance was accounted for by the correlations. The highest correlation was between the job and social rating and this was .36. The lack of higher correlations among these four ratings indicates we are assessing items that are independent of each other. This gives greater assurance that we are not talking about the same dimensions when we talk of the family rating as compared to the social rating. This also indicates that a woman may believe she is negatively affected in one life area and not in another by her drinking; and, indeed, she is probably not uniformly affected.

Background variables and interference

Since the mean score is viewed as the more precise measure of interference in any area—based as it is on a woman's response to answering the same questions—this score will be used to describe the interference in each area and to relate them to the ten background variables. In Table 4-4 the probability level for each area by the background variables is shown. Only one background variable consistently showed a significant difference: the quantity a woman drinks. The very heavy drinkers (15 or more drinks) were more likely to have a significantly higher average (mean) score in family, social, job, and health interference. The quantity a woman drinks has more recently been reported (Jones and Jones, 1976a, b) to have a different bodily effect

TABLE 4-4 *Mean Score on Interference in Family, Social, Job, and Health Areas by Background Variables*

	MEAN SCORE			
BACKGROUND VARIABLES	*Family* (4.5)	*Social* (5.7)	*Job* (4.1)	*Health* (6.5)
	PROBABILITY OF MEAN SCORE[a]			
Usual quantity of drinks	.05	.01	.05	.001
Marital and employment status	.001	NS	.01	.05
Locale (urban-suburban)	.001	.05	.01	NS
Professional status	.01	NS	NS	.001
Marital status	.001	NS	.01	NS
Age	NS	.01	NS	.05
Socioeconomic status	NS	NS	NS	.05
Race	NS	NS	NS	NS
Religion	NS	NS	NS	NS
Agency type	NS	NS	NS	NS
Total	N=150	N=150	N=126	N=150

[a] All probabilities based on F value, except the two group comparisons (urban-suburban; professional status) that used t values. The Student Newman-Keuls range test was used to compare all possible pairs of group means.

for women than for men, even when they are of the same body weight. Thus, this variable may have considerably more meaning for women than for men.

The combination variable of marital and employment status shows a significant relationship to interference in three life areas. Generally the not married–not currently employed had significantly higher mean scores, reflecting interference in the work and health areas. The currently married women scored significantly higher on family-related interference. This is to be expected, since the family area is heavily weighted with questions for the married women and it is not an adequate measure of interference for those who never married. No difference was found on interference in social relations by this variable.

The urban-suburban variable revealed that the urban women report greater interference in three areas: family, social relations, and job functioning. No difference is found in the health area. Thus, the urban woman is likely to arrive at treatment with considerably more interference than the suburban woman.

The women's professional status as a variable shows no difference in the social or work areas, but women in occupations classified as nonprofessional report greater family and health problems. The relationship between marital status and interference in family relations and job functioning is touched on above in discussing the combined variable of marriage and employment, and it is also reflected in significant differences for marital status when examined separately. The currently married have greater interference in the family area, while the never married experience greater difficulty in job functioning.

The variable of age shows those under 40 doing poorly in the social and health areas; this is due most likely to the interrelationship with some of the other background variables, especially marital status and the quantity a woman drinks, that is, they are somewhat less likely to be married and more likely to be heavier drinkers. It is not surprising that the lowest socioeconomic group has a significantly higher score on health interference, since generally all previous research reports the health of those with less income to be poorer.

Race, religion, and type of agency attended show no significant relationships with the four areas in which the interference was measured. The fact that there are no significant differences in interference by the type of treatment agency may be a factor to which we should give more attention. What it seems to mean is that outpatients, including members of AA, have similar interference to those admitted as inpatients for treatment of a drinking problem. Based on this study group and the measures cited here, inpatient treatment is not being received by those with family, social, job, and health problems that are any more pervasive.

It appears that the quantity a woman drinks should be viewed as a key variable in the alcoholism of women, but one that is probably not unique to women alcoholics. It has also been identified by others as an important variable for men. Yet we need different cutting points for what constitutes heavy and very heavy drinking for women as compared to men of the same body height both in research studies and in the world of drinking women.

Obviously, knowledge of the amount of alcohol consumed by itself does not determine if the individual is an alcoholic. As stressed in the previous chapter, a number of the study women who usually drink four or fewer drinks are in treatment for alcoholism. What is being said, however, is that based on the quantity consumed, there are differing consequences. In addition, not all alcoholic women either consume the same quantity or have the same consequences with the same degree of severity. The amount consumed, however, has a direct bearing on the consequences.

Conclusions

Many introductions are "fitting," but there may be less agreement about the "fit" of the conclusions. This chapter is no exception. A wealth of data, diverse and far ranging, is presented. It is clear that once drinking becomes problematic the women seem highly aware of the differing norms that exist for them in contrast to men who are heavy drinkers. Most perceive women, such as themselves, who drink heavily as more rejected than men. This may account for why so many drift away from friends and social activities.

The effect of heavy drinking on the sexual behavior of women is explored, and the data lend credence both to increased sexual satisfaction existing for some women after drinking and to decreased interest for others. Heavy drinking affects the sexual behavior of some of the women.

The background variables permitted looking at the consequences of drinking by the different subgroups of women. Many of these findings are of some substantive interest especially for treating alcoholic women. A woman's area of residence reflects a number of these differences. Suburban women subjectively experience significantly more criticism about their heavy drinking. The measure of their emotional health, however, shows no difference between urban and suburban women. In addition, no difference exists in the physical health problems the study women present by area of residence. This means that women entering treatment for alcoholism in both city and suburban communities are experiencing equally the consequences of drinking in their physical and emotional health. This finding is probably universal for alcoholic women admitted to treatment and can be addressed early as a direct result of their drinking.

Some of the variations noted by the other background variables also merit comment, especially as they relate to the scales measuring interference in the four areas of family and social life, work, and physical health. All four areas, plus the women's emotional health and their trouble score, relate significantly to the quantity of alcohol consumed. The very heavy drinkers (usually more than 15 drinks) show significantly more interference in all the areas measured. Consumption alone can be viewed as a meaningful clue to the extensive consequences of drinking. If a woman is at the highest level in the quantity she drinks, it is likely that there is already pervasive disturbance in every facet of living. Likely, too, social, family, and work relations are already strained if not severed and there is need for an alteration in the consumption patterns in order to obtain change in the effected areas.

Notes
1. The concept of troubles discussed here is distinguished from the previous section, which involved the spontaneous response of women to an open-ended question. As discussed in this section, "troubles" are specific questions asked of each woman.
2. Johnson, et al. report their definition of heavier drinkers as translated into an index of blood alcohol content (BAC). This index corrects for the average difference in weight between men and women, since the authors recognize the same amount would have a greater effect for a woman than a man. As interpreted in the text of their paper (pp. 36–37) and the appendix (C), a male of average weight taking two drinks a day obtains a score

of .04 on the BAC index. A female of average weight with 1.5 drinks a day would also have a score of .04 on the BAC. Both men and women would then be categorized as heavier drinkers. This level defines the *lower* limit of the heavier drinking categories and, of course, could be higher. The authors note that heavier by their definitions is not equivalent to excessive or that which is used for legal intoxication, which *begins* at the .08 blood alcohol level.

5
Marriages, Children, and Husbands

Summary of findings

The norm for most of these women is to be married at least once.

The majority of those who were ever separated or divorced do not consider a drinking-related problem to be the major reason for the separation or divorce. When they do, as many view their husband's heavy drinking as the main reason as do those who only blame their own drinking.

Just over two-fifths (43 percent) of the women who were ever married are currently married. For most of the women currently living with their husbands, it is their first marriage.

It is a rare husband who does not drink with his wife. At the same time, most husbands are reported to disapprove of their wife's drinking.

Only seven husbands actually left their wives because of heavy drinking. This represents 7 percent of those study women who ever married and casts grave doubt on the belief that husbands are more likely than wives to leave an alcoholic spouse.

A high percentage of the women who appear for treatment have good awareness of their difficulty in functioning, especially as wife and mother.

Husbands were also interviewed. These interviews support the reports of the women in a number of areas. Yet, the large number of husbands characterizing their sexual relationship as poor may come as a surprise to many of the women.

The incidence of having a child with a birth defect is high but may be independent of "heavy drinking."

Almost three-fourths of the women who ever had children believe their own drinking has had a negative impact on one or more of their children.

The questions sometimes raised about women who become alcoholic are often associated with their marital status. If they are or have been married, the question is often asked whether their heavy drinking is due to an unsatisfactory marriage? If they remain single or begin heavy drinking after divorce, is such drinking the result of loneliness and society's poor assimilation of the single woman?

Usually, too, there is an expectation for most marriages to result in the birth of children. Thus, the woman marrying assumes first the role of wife and then, traditionally, the role of mother. A further question, which is asked about women who drink heavily, becomes most germane when pregnancy and child birth are discussed. It is no longer a matter of simply assaying the consequences of drinking for the woman's marriage; a more disturbing question has to do with whether heavy drinking negatively affects childbearing. In this regard three major questions are often raised: Is there a greater likelihood that heavy-drinking women will not conceive? If they do conceive, is there a greater likelihood of miscarriages? And if they carry to term, is there a greater likelihood of birth defects, such as lowered birth weight, heart defects, brain damage, and so on? This is now a matter of great interest and is a research area receiving increasing attention as reflected in recent reviews of the literature on the fetal alcohol syndrome (Streissguth, 1976; Martin, 1977). The part played by men who drink heavily in fetal and birth defects has yet to receive more than passing scientific attention. Recently, questions have arisen about infant withdrawal, questions directed more frequently in the past at women who are on hard drugs. In addition to these areas, the effect of heavy drinking on a woman's rearing of her children is also addressed in the present study.

Because studies of alcoholic women are still so rare, basic questions about the interaction between spouses and their drinking are explored. In the past, many questions have been raised in relation to this interaction: Did the husband introduce the wife to heavy drinking? Is the husband, too, a heavy drinker? Does he somehow perpetuate the wife's heavy drinking, and does he then interfere with her obtaining help for herself or, alternately, not facilitate treatment? And, finally, is he more likely to leave her because of her drinking? Whenever husbands were seen, we also asked their perception of the development of their wife's problem drinking.

Marriage
STABILITY OF MARRIAGE

The norm for most of these women is to be married at least once. Even though they may not now be married, the majority (72 percent) have had a legal marriage. Those who had never married came primarily from urban treatment centers.

The marriages of the women cannot be considered enduring. At the time they were seen, just as many were separated (11 percent) or divorced (19 percent) as were currently married (31 percent). A number of the women, too, were already widows (11 percent). The remaining women had not married (27 percent) at the time of the interview. Of those who ever married, a little over two-fifths (42 percent) are now separated or divorced, a figure exceeding the high reported for recent marriages.[1]

Only a very small number of women (9 percent) have had more than one marriage—with three women having married three times and one four times. Where there were multiple marriages, divorce was the characteristic outcome; for most of the women currently living with their husbands, it was their first marriage. Three were in a second marriage and one in a fourth.

For only a handful of women did the disruption of their marriage take place in the year just prior to their coming for treatment. For many of those who were ever separated, divorced, or widowed, this was not a recent event; it occurred as much as 6 or more years previous for some 52 percent of these women.

Of the women who ever married, more than a fourth (27 percent) did not drink heavily during their marriage; almost one-half (46 percent) are now in the marriage which is their first and in which they drink heavily; about one-fourth, too, drank heavily during a marriage now ended by separation or divorce.

Omitting widowhood, an event apparently unrelated to the woman's drinking problem, and considering only those women who were ever separated or divorced, many (43 percent) acknowledge there were *signs* of their drinking problems at the time of separation or divorce. Yet the majority (61 percent) did not believe their drinking problem was the major reason. When drinking was mentioned, just as many viewed their husband's heavy drinking as the main reason for the separation or divorce as did those who acknowledged their own drinking behavior as playing a part.

Some 18 percent of the women who ever married stated their husband either left them or asked them to leave at some point in the marriage because of their heavy drinking. Yet only seven husbands, representing 7 percent of those who ever married, actually left their wives because of heavy drinking. Such a finding seems to cast grave doubt on the belief that husbands are more likely than wives to leave an alcoholic spouse.[2] Yet the relationships in marriages in which separation was threatened were extremely contentious, filled with blaming and with sex withheld, at times by the husband and sometimes by the wife because of her drinking. Typical replies by the study women are:

My husband doesn't want anything to do with me.

He is critical of me, is never home and I know he is cheating.

Whenever I do something he doesn't like, he locks me out of the bedroom; he calls me names in front of the kids and he beats me up. He tells me I'm a tramp, an alcoholic, an unfit mother, no good.

[As to sex] I would not know what was happening and did not want to be near him. I slept on the couch.

CHARACTERISTICS OF THE WOMEN BY MARITAL STATUS

The women's marital status was found to vary significantly by a number of their background characteristics: age, race, professional status, socioeconomic status, marital and employment status, and area of residence (Chapter 2). Few of the currently married women are likely to be professional women (26 percent). Approximately two-fifths of the married women are in the highest socioeconomic group. About a third (32 percent) of the married women are also employed. The currently married women are predominantly suburban (72 percent), and almost all are white (90 percent).

HEAVY DRINKING MARRIAGES: THE HUSBAND

Less than one in ten of the women who themselves drank heavily during their marriage described their husbands as abstainers. This proportion indicates fewer abstainers than the national data suggest as the norm for men (Cahalan, Cisin, and Crossley, 1969). Thus, the women in this study seem more likely to have married drinking men. If the husband did drink alcoholic beverages, he was almost equally likely to be described by the wife as either a fairly heavy or heavy drinker (42 percent) as he was a fairly light drinker (48 percent).[3] The remaining women (10 percent) could not designate either of these categories to describe their husbands' drinking.

Drinking together was quite common; it was a rare husband who did not drink with his wife during their marriage in which the woman drank heavily. Almost a third of the women also acknowledge that they "got drunk together." Some 20 percent also believe that their husbands' drinking tended to influence their own drinking pattern by increasing their intake; only three women believe their husbands' drinking had a positive effect in that they tended to drink less.

As they describe their marriage during their heavy drinking period, less than a third of the women believe their husband also had a drinking problem. This is somewhat less than might be expected. Despite this low estimate by the study women, a sizable number of these husbands (two out of five) obtained treatment for a drinking problem. This percentage is relatively high since national estimates suggest that only about 1 in 10 persons obtains treatment for drinking-related problems. Obviously, the reporting of a drinking problem either by a spouse or by a significant other can be faulted, since the respondent may not be an objective observer and the definition of a drinking problem is subjective. Yet the number of husbands who obtained treatment for drinking would seem to lend support to the study women's responses.

Almost without exception, heavy drinking began for the study women after their marriage. This obviously does not imply a cause-and-effect relationship but rather tells more about the timing of such a problem for women. A similar finding is reported for national treatment centers (Armor, Polich, and Stambul, 1976). It is not surprising, then, that the vast number of these study women describe their marriages generally as "not too happy" or frankly "unhappy." What is surprising is that as many as 37 percent say their marriages are "happy" or "very happy."

Although the women are frequently married to men who drink—and many of them heavily—these wives are conscious of disapproval by their husbands of their own heavy drinking. Seventy-seven describe their husbands' attitudes as disapproving, with relatively few believing their husbands accepted their heavy drinking.

ROLE OF WIFE AND MOTHER

Obviously the two roles of wife and mother most frequently associated with women are not synonymous. Yet, the woman's functioning in each of these areas is of great interest and increased understanding may give insights in planning early treatment intervention. Towards the end of the interview, each of the study women was handed a booklet that contained a series of statements on family relations to which she was asked to respond "yes" or "no." For example, her role as wife: "I have had difficulty some of the time in my role of wife because of drinking." "I cannot or could not carry out my role as a wife because of drinking." In her role as mother: "I have or had difficulty some of the time in caring for my children because of drinking." "I cannot or could not carry out my role of mother because of drinking."

A majority of the women (57 percent) who were ever married stated they had difficulty in their role as "wife." Those who believe they were unable to carry out this role accounted for somewhat less (44 percent) of the ever-married women. While a high proportion acknowledging difficulty in this role is expected, these figures also tell us that many of the women appearing for treatment have a good awareness of their difficulty in functioning. Such preexisting awareness can well be used to involve the entire family in therapy.

As we indicated, similar profiles were drawn of the study women in their mothering role. While fewer report difficulty functioning as mothers than they do as wives, a substantial number acknowledge not only difficulty in fulfilling the mothering role (42 percent) but an inability to perform that role at all (32 percent). We will discuss these findings in some detail shortly.

Children
PREGNANCY AND BIRTH DEFECTS

Interest in the fetal alcohol syndrome has been high since it was widely reported in the literature and media in the early 1970s. It is now known that ethanol crosses the placenta. Warner and Rosset (1975) summarize well the history of this phenomena. In a descriptive, and retrospective interview such as the present, the questions asked of the study women were limited to probing for birth defects. The women were asked if they drank heavily during any of their pregnancies, if any of their children were born with defects, and if they drank heavily during that particular pregnancy. Slightly more than a third of the women were never pregnant. Those who had ever been pregnant were asked also how the pregnancies affected their drinking. More than half (56 percent) stated they did not drink during a pregnancy. This decision may or may not have been related to the pregnancy. An additional fourth (27 percent) did not alter their drinking patterns. Some women drank less (3 percent) while others (7 percent) drank an increased amount. Information is lacking on the remaining women.

Thus, 16 women drank heavily during a pregnancy. Three of those reported having children with birth defects. This can be compared with the 76 women who did not drink heavily during their pregnancy, eight of whom reported having children with birth defects. The defects reported include congenital heart defects, cleft palate, cleft lip, blindness, and a kidney problem. Having a child with a birth defect tends to be slightly higher among women who reported heavy drinking during pregnancy (19 percent) as compared with those (11 percent) who did not drink heavily. The data from this study does not lend support, or even rebut, recent explorations of the existence of a causal relationship between chronic heavy drinking and birth defects. Yet, the proportion of *all* these women, now in treatment for alcoholism, who ever became pregnant and reported having children with birth defects does seem high and to be independent of their own heavy drinking during pregnancy. Reports on birth defects for all pregnant women is not firmly known since there is no centralized nationwide registry.[4] It may be that some women who subsequently become alcoholic have a higher proportion of children with birth defects, and it also may be that such anomalies at birth can be traced to any number of other factors, either genetic or situational, and not linked causally to heavy drinking.

CHILDREN AND THEIR PROBLEMS

The study women had an average of 2.7 children, slightly higher than the national norm of 2.09. At the time of the interview the average age of the firstborn children was 19 while that of the last born children was 13. One-third of the women with children reported that at least one child has at some time had learning problems. Over one-half also reported difficulties with school attendance, and more than one-third of the women stated that they were contacted by school authorities regarding problems with their children. Such problems, of course, cannot be causally related to the woman's heavy drinking. Yet Haberman (1966) provides data to support the higher frequency of occurrence of such problems among children of alcoholic parents.

However, responses of a smaller number of non-alcoholic sisters to the same questions about their own children (described later) do not reveal any differences between the children on the questions relating to school and child behavior.

In most cases in which there is more than one child in the home the children are said to get along well with each other; in only 13 percent of the families are there reports of frequent quarreling and fighting among the children.

MOTHERING

Most of the women are primarily responsible for the care of their children and have no other adult help. For only 20 percent of the women who became mothers has someone else cared for their children for most of the children's lives, most usually a relative or, in two instances, the children's father. Four of the women have had children in the care of social agencies. Thirty-nine percent report their children have been separated from them at some point in their lives. These separations, of course, are not entirely the direct result of the women's drinking, but many were prolonged because of it. Fourteen children were separated for from 1 to 7 months, 15 from 1 to 5 years, and 9 were separated for 8 or more years. In spite of this rather high percentage of separation, only eight women had children placed by the court as the result of a negligence charge.

It is obvious that self-reports by parents of how their own behavior affects their children is especially suspect in its validity. Parents may either exaggerate or underestimate the effects of their own behavior, and because of this, they may be less than objective observers of their children. Aware of this limitation, we first asked the study women a series of descriptive questions about their pregnancies and then about the development of their children. Finally, we asked three questions about the children which specifically related to the woman's own drinking; we also asked them to respond to a number of descriptive phrases about the effects of their drinking on their children. The questions were:

1. In general, are there some specific aspects of being a mother that may have suffered because of your drinking?
2. Have the children witnessed quarrels or fights as a result of drinking?
3. Have the children ever talked to you about (your) drinking? Would you say: "often," "sometimes," "never"? If "often" or "sometimes," what did they say?

In response to the first question, more than half (56 percent) of the women believe their mothering was negatively affected by their drinking. This figure is considerably higher than the 42 percent having difficulty in *caring* for their children. The women most frequently believe they were not giving enough attention to the children. Several women also reported placing too much responsibility on the children or described a great deal of tension at home because of their drinking. A small number of the women were also quite aware that their children became upset by their drinking.

In answer to the second question, in two-thirds of the families the children are said to have witnessed quarrels or fights in the home as a result of drinking. While not unexpected, such a finding lends support to the disruptiveness of heavy drinking on family relationships.

As to the third question asked, even more of the women, three-fourths, reported their children speaking to them about their drinking. Mostly the children asked them to stop or to reduce their drinking; relatively few children were described as openly critical or as actually removing liquor from the home. Almost half of the women say they drink with their adult children, but the majority also indicate they are aware of their children's disapproval of their drinking.

In order to obtain a further assessment of how a woman's drinking affected her children, a card containing the descriptive phrases shown below was given to her. She was then asked to select whichever statement applies to *each* of her children.

EFFECTS ON CHILDREN

1. *Almost none.* Child not aware of my drinking, and I was always able to do what had to be done for a child.
2. *Probably some effect.* Child may have been (or was) aware of my drinking; child sometimes seemed upset by my drinking; I couldn't always do what had to be done for the child.
3. *Quite a bit affected.* Child is (or was) aware of my drinking. Child seemed upset by my drinking, asked me to stop drinking. Frequently, I couldn't do what had to be done for the child.

Most of the women report some effect on their children because of their drinking. As seen in Table 5–1 30 percent of the women believe their children were unaffected by their drinking.

One of the major differences by birth order is when there is only one child. In such instances the women (52 percent) are least likely to report a child as being affected. As the number of children increases beyond one, a smaller and somewhat similar percentage of children is reported as *not* affected by the mother's drinking, ranging from 18 percent to 30 percent. Yet those women with two children reported just over three-fifths of their children as being affected. As

TABLE 5-1 *Women's Self-Report of Any Effects on Children from Their Drinking by Number of Children Reared: Percentage Distribution*

NUMBER OF CHILDREN AFFECTED[a]	NUMBER OF CHILDREN REARED					
	Total[b] (N=98)	One (N=23)	Two (N=28)	Three (N=20)	Four (N=17)	Five or more[c] (N=10)
None	30	52	18	25	24	30
One	21	48	21	10	6	10
Two	28	—	61	20	29	10
Three	10	—	—	45	6	—
Four	7	—	—	—	35	10
Five or more	4	—	—	—	—	40

[a] "Some effect" or "quite a bit affected" was combined; of those women with children affected, the majority responded "some effect" (60 percent) as compared to "quite a bit affected" (40 percent).
[b] The total here includes three women with adopted children and one with a stepchild; it excludes two women who did not rear their children (death of a child and husband caring for child since birth).
[c] Four women had five children, three had seven, two had eight and one had nine.

the number of children in a family increases, there is less likelihood of such a high percentage of *all* the children being affected.

A number of significant differences emerge in the background characteristics of the study women who described the differing effects of drinking on their children; three variables show significant differences: marital and employment status, race, and suburban-urban residence. Differences approaching significance ($p < .06$) were in marital status, age, and socioeconomic status. The direction of each of these findings will be discussed briefly.

Black women were less likely ($p < .001$) than white women to report their drinking to have some effect on their children. Since significantly more of the black women described someone else as the prime caretaker of their children, we omitted this group of women from the analysis, but the significant relationship persisted. Unexpected differences were found by marital status. Married women still living with their husbands were more likely to report some effect on their children. When analyzed by the marital and employment status variable, both the employed and unemployed married women reported higher and similar proportions of their children affected by their drinking, as compared to those not currently married. The suburban women were significantly more likely to have children (86 percent) than the urban women (51 percent). More of the suburban mothers stated their drinking affected their children.

Fewer study women under 30 are likely to have had children. Those who are mothers viewed their children as less affected by their drinking. This may be accounted for by their shorter period of problem drinking. The women who are more than 50 years of age also are more likely to have reported fewer of their children as being affected. This, too, may be the result of their children's age when they began their problem drinking, or even of the greater likelihood of the children being out of the home. Thus, more of the women between the ages of 30 through 49 reported drinking to have some effect on their children.

More women in the highest socioeconomic group have no children, but when they do, they are just as likely to describe their drinking as affecting their children as the women in the middle socioeconomic group. In fact, a smaller proportion of women in the lower socioeconomic group reported their drinking affecting their children, and this is almost a significant difference ($p < .06$).

Despite the large number of women indicating awareness of the negative impact of their drinking on one or more of their children, over one-half described their relationship with their children as very good. One-third reported their relationship as fairly good. Only 13 percent of the women said it is not good or poor. In families where the husband is also present in the home, just over one-half are described by the women as also having a very good relationship with their children, one-fourth say fairly good and slightly more than one-fifth (22 percent) say it is not good or poor. The women usually characterized the husbands' relationships with the children as less satisfactory than their own. Only those study women who described their own relationships with a child as poor tend to view their husbands' as better.

Husband interviews

At the time that the initial interviews with the 150 women were completed, we had seen a total of 47 women who were married and living with their husbands. We requested permission to interview their husbands, and 33 of the 47 women agreed to our conducting such an interview. The most frequent reason given for withholding permission related to the poor marital relationship.

Of these 33 husbands, we subsequently were able to interview 20. One had died, two couples had already separated and divorce proceedings were in process, four husbands did not respond to our repeated efforts to contact them, and six refused either directly or through their wives. Although only a small number of husbands were seen, these interviews do provide some insight into the perceptions of husbands of alcoholic women. We were also interested in determining if the views expressed by the husband in a number of areas supported those of the wife and also hoped to gain understanding of the development of the wife's alcoholism. This is obviously not a representative group of the spouses of alcoholic women.

PERCEPTION OF THE TIMING OF THE PROBLEM

There was uniform agreement concerning when heavy drinking became a problem. Nineteen of the husbands and their wives independently traced drinking as a problem to a point after their marriage. The one remaining couple saw the problem as worsening in the year that the marriage took place, but heavy drinking was present prior to the marriage.

HELP-SEEKING BY HUSBANDS

The large majority of the husbands (16) interviewed had taken steps to intervene in the problems of their wives by seeking outside help. Among the resources consulted were psychiatrists, AA groups, hospitals, social agencies, physicians, and a minister. Some couples were clearly seeking help from more than one source in the course of their search for treatment, but psychiatrists and AA groups were most frequently mentioned. Although all the husbands recognized a problem, many—even those who actively sought help—had not considered alcoholism. In fact, 8 of the 20 husbands interviewed said they did not realize alcoholism was the problem, and 3 of the 8 at first thought their wives required psychiatric care.

I went with her to a psychiatrist, a social agency, and finally AA. I didn't realize she was an alcoholic.

I never went for help before AA. I didn't realize how involved she was in liquor.

I never saw her as an alcoholic. She was under psychiatric care, but those birds don't tell you much.

THE HUSBAND'S UNDERSTANDING OF ALCOHOLISM

We systematically addressed a husband's perceptions of critical incidents leading to his wife's alcoholism and will discuss them shortly. During the interview, however, some husbands volunteered their own explanations about the cause of alcoholism in their wives. Such explanations were not uniformly elicited, but they are worth noting since such views may have affected the ways in which these husbands reponded to a drinking problem.

I see it as a chemical disturbance.

I saw it as a violent personality change due to medication.

I see it as a lack of control and discipline.

I see it as related to her anger with me.

I didn't see the problem as drinking just that something was wrong with her.

All the husbands said that once they recognized alcoholism was the problem, they could not accept it. Fifteen of the 20 husbands said they disapproved and were openly critical of their wives. Five of them said they disapproved but were less clear in their reactions. Several felt helpless and said or did nothing to intervene.

MARRIAGES BETWEEN ALCOHOLIC SPOUSES

Each husband was asked to characterize and describe his own drinking. Of the 20 husbands seen, 3 described themselves as "heavy" drinkers, 5 as "fairly heavy," 11 as light drinkers, and 1 as a nondrinker. Thus eight of the husbands interviewed were heavy drinkers and five of these eight characterized themselves as having a drinking problem. Only 12 couples agreed on the description of the husband's drinking: The disagreement was in the direction of the husbands tending to describe their own drinking as "heavier" than did their wives. In contrast, five women stated their husbands had treatment for drinking, while only three of these five husbands acknowledged such an occurrence.

PERCEPTION OF DEVELOPMENT OF DRINKING
PROBLEMS IN THE STUDY WOMEN

The first specific question asked the husbands about the onset of the woman's drinking problem. Did the onset occur in a critical situation that could be viewed as contributing to or as precipitating a drinking problem. The same question was asked of the couples. Although 11 women and 12 of their husbands could offer a situational reason for the onset of the problem drinking, virtually none agreed on the specific event except for two couples, one of whom agreed that a death and the second of whom concurred that their marital problems were a factor. This lack of agreement on specific situational events offers support to the earlier discussion in Chapter 3 where such a situational view of the development of alcoholism in women is challenged.

EFFECTS ON THE MARRIAGE

Other portions of the interview dealt with the effects of the wife's drinking upon the marital relationship. Of the 20 couples interviewed, 6 had separated at some point during the course of their marriage, and 3 of the husbands attributed these separations to their wife's drinking. In addition, one husband suggested his wife's frequent attendance at AA meetings was the reason for separation; two described separations as occurring prior to the development of the wife's drinking problem. In all, however, most of the husbands interviewed (15) acknowledged they *considered* separating, not an unexpected finding in marriages with an alcoholic spouse. Disagreement was high between husbands and wives on whether or not the husbands either left or threatened to leave because of drinking. For example, six husbands said they did make such threats, but their wives did not concur. This may well indicate that the alcoholic woman represses such threats or possibly because of an alcohol-related loss of memory, known as a blackout, does not recall such a threat.

Both partners in the marriage were asked how they would characterize the relationship. Thirteen of the 20 couples agreed in their assessment; seven described the relationship as happy, and six as unhappy. In the other seven marriages, there was disagreement, without any clear direction to these disagreements.

SEXUAL RELATIONSHIPS

While most of the husbands (13) found their wives drinking interfered with their sexual relationship, only four women believed this was the case. Thus most of the currently married couples perceive their sexual life in quite different terms. The husbands say:

She's frigid—drinking contributes to it.

Sure drinking interferes—she has no desire, no ability, no energy.

Sure drinking interferes—she gets zonked.

It's bad sexually.

Yes, drinking interferes, it makes me feel like I'm going to bed with a prostitute. I can't stand the smell.

It has affected our sex—a real turn-off.

In contrast, some speak positively of the sexual relationship:

Our marriage is bad. The only satisfaction is our sex life.

My only satisfaction is our love life.

I see her as basically frigid, and she is more relaxed during sex when she is drunk.

Extramarital relations are not a rare occurrence for the husbands—4 out of 10 acknowledge an extramarital relationship, and this can be assumed to be a conservative figure. Two attribute this directly to their wife's drinking. While this seems like a high proportion of husbands (40 percent) having extramarital affairs, it possibly is more a commentary on the occurrence of extramarital affairs during marriage than on alcoholism in women. Only one of the eight husbands said this was a current involvement; unfortunately, we did not ask these same questions of the women. Research by Kinsey et al. (1948)

and Hunt (1974) point to up to 50 percent of married men having intercourse with women other than their wives at some time.

PERSISTING IN MARRIAGE

Why does a husband continue in the marriage? Perhaps the reasons for persisting are similar, if not the same, for a man as for a woman who is married to an alcoholic. A notable difference, however, did emerge. The husbands never cited financial dependency as a reason. Rather they asserted most often the needs of the children, "will power," or their continuing love for their wives. One suspects that the first two reasons are those often given by spouses when they remain in an unhappy marriage. The husband's comments are in turn, stoical, bitter, and poignant.

I said I'd love her the rest of my life; I'm a man of my word.

The children keep us together; it makes you resentful and always suspicious it will start again.

I used to have hope; no more—it's the children.

I have faith in my wife; I also care for her very much and believe that we can make it.

We have a deep love for one another, a strong bond.

I have no alternative. The children must be brought up.

THE CHILDREN

Next, we will discuss how the children fare as described by both husbands and wives. Eighteen of the couples interviewed had children. Based on their self-reports, a minimum of five of these couples can be viewed as having drinking problems; we did not attempt to assess the singular and possibly differential effects on the children in cases where both parents are alcoholics.

Agreement is quite high between the couples about the children; the interviews with the husbands support the women's view that a high proportion of the children are negatively affected by their drinking. The husbands were asked questions similar to those used to interview their wives:

How often did your wife have difficulty taking care of the children because of her drinking? Often? Sometimes? Never?

Have the children witnessed quarrels or fights as a result of drinking? Often? Sometimes? Never?

Are there some specific aspects of your wife's being a mother that may have suffered because of her drinking?

Have the children ever talked to you about their mother's drinking? Often? Sometimes? Never?

How would you rate the effect of your wife's drinking on each of the children?

Very similar proportions of the couples agreed on the presence of these various negative factors in the lives of the children. For example, 10 wives and 11 husbands acknowledged difficulty in the mother caring for the children; 13 of the 18 couples agreed on the presence or absence of child-care problems and only 5 couples disagreed. The disagreements focused essentially on whether or not the mother's drinking had a negative impact on the family. For example, in three families the wife believes there was no problem in caring for the children whereas her husband believes one did exist.

As for the specific aspects affected, eight couples agreed that diminished attention to the children was the major problem. Only three husbands noted friction as an area of concern. Two wives believe that no aspect of their mothering was affected. This view is not shared by their husbands.

The children witnessing quarrels and/or fights because of drinking is a fairly universal experience in 14 of the 18 families. In only two instances did the couples agree this was not the case; for two others there was disagreement.

While most of the children spoke to both parents at some point about their mother's drinking, they were more likely to speak to the mothers directly (15) than they were to their fathers (12).

There is substantial agreement by mothers and fathers about the effects on the 50 children who were rated. Of the 39 judgments that agree, most (32) contend that the children were negatively affected; the remaining agreements contend that the children were not affected.

Conclusions

This chapter has focused on those study women who are (or were) married, their children, and interviews with a smaller number of husbands. Although their marriages are not stable, the women quite often do not attribute this instability to their alcoholism. Those who do remain married report a high degree of dissatisfaction. The women's awareness of the negative impact of a drinking problem on their children is high, and the interviews with the husbands support this perception.

The women apparently, however, do not perceive their current marriage in the same terms as their husbands, possibly because denial was still operating at the time of these interviews. This is especially true of their sex life; the degree of negativism of husbands as they spoke of this aspect of their relationship is compelling, but yet no husband stated that he completely stopped being sexually involved with his wife because of her drinking. At the same time, extramarital relationships of the currently married men is no higher than the national norm.

The case can be made for these being the "best" of the current marriages of the study women since the reason for so many of the husbands not being interviewed is ascribed by their wives to the poor relationship. Many of the husbands who were interviewed were actively involved in seeking help for their wives, although their awareness initially of alcoholism as a problem was quite limited. Many just had a sense of "something wrong," and it was only the intervention of others that established alcohol as the problem. Yet, because of the small and selective number of husbands interviewed, these inferences must be viewed as tentative.

These data tell us little about the actual effects on children. Only longitudinal studies with control groups can answer the question whether or not children with mothers who are problem drinkers have demonstrably greater difficulties in their development and eventual functioning than do other children.

One is left with the feeling that the data support well the tragedy of the life of the alcoholic woman and offer the most persuasive reasons to date for a clear acknowledgment of this problem of women. We have not discussed the "single woman" separately in this study.

One suspects that she affects less the lives of others, unless she is involved in a close relationship or lives with someone.

The data presented in this chapter have not been obtained systematically for alcoholic men as husbands and fathers; such an important area obviously requires more extensive study. Most likely, a more detailed analysis and comparison between alcoholic mothers and alcoholic fathers and the effects of their drinking on their children could be best pursued in longitudinal studies. Such a study (Miller and Jang, 1977) focusing on children of alcoholics from lower-class, multiproblem urban families reports the results of a twenty-year longitudinal study. The findings, though limited to a lower-class population and not representative of alcoholic parents, are of considerable interest. For example, these authors note that *not all children* of alcoholic parents themselves become alcoholic or "social failures." They hypothesize that a good socialization experience can mitigate a history of parental alcoholism. After studying the socialization experiences of the children of alcoholics from multi-problem families, the authors conclude that alcoholism of a parent lessens the likelihood that a child will achieve a trouble-free adulthood. Of more interest, however, is the authors' speculation regarding escape routes, which they define as the ways children are able to overcome the influence of their background, for example, a good marriage, a good education, a job with opportunities for self-enhancement, a change in life style. Such avenues, of course, are often opened only by chance.

Notes

1. A very similar percentage of separated and divorced women (44 percent) of the ever-married women is reported for those women treated at National Alcoholism Treatment Centers (Armor, Polich, and Stambul, 1976). The United States Bureau of the Census data for 1975 report that of those women born between 1900 and 1959, 17 percent of those who married have been divorced at least once; in contrast, it is projected that 33 percent of recent first marriages will end in divorce.
2. No comparative data is available on the question as posed here for wives of male alcoholics, although it is believed that women are more likely to remain in their marriages because of financial dependency.
3. The 81 women who drank heavily during their marriage were first asked if their husbands drank. If they did, the women were then asked: "Which

most closely describes your husband's drinking? Fairly light? Fairly heavy? Heavy?"

4. More than 200,000 infants are born with structural or metabolic disorders each year; another 50,000 have markedly low birth weight. Paul Ma, statistician for the National Foundation/March of Dimes, estimates these infants to represent 7 percent to 8 percent of the newborn. The data for this present study did not include questions specifically about low birth weight, miscarriages, and so on. (See *Facts: 1977,* The National Foundation/March of Dimes.)

6
The Family in the Etiology of Alcoholism

Summary of findings
The data may well reflect changing norms in previous generations of parents: Only 3 percent of the women over 50 as compared to 55 percent of those under 30 reported seeing their mother drunk. In contrast, a considerably higher percentage of fathers have been seen drunk by women in each age group, but again those under 30 report the highest percentage (89 percent).

Almost two-fifths (39 percent) also reported one or more parents have a drinking problem. In addition, 13 percent reported a sister with a drinking problem, and 32 percent have at least one brother with a drinking problem. In all, 61 percent of the women have one or more relatives with a drinking problem.

We interviewed 33 of the non-alcoholic sisters, and we were able to compare 86 of the study women with their non-alcoholic sisters on a number of critical points.

Interviews with the non-alcoholic sisters supported the women's description of parental drinking and drunkenness.

In addition:

Significantly more of the sisters are currently married, although no differences are found in the proportion who were married at some point.

More of the alcoholic women use tranquilizers than their non-alcoholic sisters, supporting the higher and dangerous combining of tranquilizers with alcohol by alcoholic women.

Using a scale to measure emotional health most of the non-alcoholic sisters fall within the "normal" range in contrast to alcoholic women, the majority of whom have a high degree of psychiatric symptomatology as they entered treatment.

Most of the sisters drink but in fairly light quantities, and they drink primarily for social reasons.

Many of the sisters (70 percent) believe drinking women are more rejected socially than men, but even more of the alcoholic study women believe this to be so.

Alcoholic women experienced their parents differently than their non-alcoholic sisters. It remains moot whether or not this finding lends support to role confusion as the basis for alcoholism in women.

The work of Anderson summarized here on the sex-role identification of the matched sisters does not support the earlier findings of Wilsnack that alcoholic women are more masculine than non-alcoholic women in unconscious identification.

Among women and men who are alcoholics, regardless of their country of origin, the rates of alcoholism among their relatives appear to be high (Cotton, 1979). Studies of women alcoholics give much attention to their family background and to the incidence of problem drinking in their parental histories. Estimates of the incidence of alcoholism in fathers of alcoholic women ranges from 23 percent to 51 percent (Wood, 1966; Mulford, 1977). The incidence of alcoholism in mothers of women alcoholics range from 3 percent to 12 percent (Winokur and Clayton, 1968; Mulford, 1977).

When men and women alcoholics are compared, it is consistently reported that women are more likely to have members of the family who are alcoholic. Lisansky (1957) stated that 44 percent of the women and 35 percent of the men in her sample had a history of parental problem drinking. Sherfey (1955) evaluated 161 alcoholics, 72 of whom were women, and found that 68 percent of the women as compared to 44 percent of the men came from homes where alcoholism was found. Mulford (1977) reports that 62 percent of the women and 41 percent of the men in his study have one or more alcoholic family members. Men and women were equally likely (3 percent) to have an alcoholic mother, but a slightly higher proportion of women than men had an alcoholic father (23 percent compared to 17 percent).

In the present study, information was obtained on both parental attitudes toward drinking as well as parental drinking behavior. Sixty percent of the subjects describe their fathers as approving of drinking, and 83 percent report their fathers to be drinkers. Perhaps the most significant finding about paternal drinking is that 20 percent of the subjects recall *sometimes* seeing their fathers drunk, and 31 percent recall *often* seeing their fathers drunk. Thus, it is not uncommon for the women to have seen their fathers drunk, and with 51 percent reporting such an occurrence, this incidence of witnessing frequent paternal drunkenness seems high. Of considerable interest is the finding that paternal drunkenness varies with the age of the subject ($p < .001$). Seventy-three percent of the 22 study women whose fathers do not drink at all are age 40 or older, while 89 percent of the study women under age 30 report having seen their father drunk sometimes or often.

Although fewer mothers than fathers (37 percent) are said to approve of drinking, 59 percent of the mothers drink. Drunkenness is reported for considerably fewer mothers than fathers. Fourteen percent of the subjects recall *sometimes* seeing their mothers drunk, and 9 percent recall *often* seeing their mothers drunk. Black subjects are more likely than white subjects to have mothers who do not drink at all, and they are thus less likely to have ever seen their mothers drunk ($p < .05$).

As with paternal drunkenness, maternal drunkenness varies inversely with the age of the women; the older the woman, the less likely she is to have a drinking mother. Similarly, the younger the woman, the greater likelihood that she has seen her mother drunk sometimes or often ($p < .001$). This finding may well reflect changing norms. The data are striking: Only 3 percent of the women 50 and older reported seeing their mothers drunk, whereas 55 percent of those under 30 stated this occurred. This is probably easily explained by the changing prevalence of maternal drinking over time. For example, 64 percent of the study women now 50 or older reported mothers as abstainers while only 15 percent of those under 30 reported mothers as abstainers.

A total of 58 percent of the subjects have a history of parental drunkenness: 36 percent have seen only their fathers drunk, 7 percent only their mothers, and 15 percent reported having seen both parents drunk. When asked specifically about problem drinking in their parents, approximately 39 percent believe that one or both parents have a drinking problem: 7 percent stated that only their mother has a drinking problem; 27 percent stated that only their father does, and 5 percent stated that both parents have a drinking problem. Yet, in view of the data gathered on parental drunkenness, this perception of parental problem drinking may be highly conservative. For example, while 15 percent reported having seen both parents drunk sometimes or often, only 5 percent stated that both parents have a drinking problem. Because these data were obtained as the women entered treatment—a time when most knew relatively little about alcoholism—the point at which they responded may easily explain this perception.

In contrast to Lisansky's homogeneous study group (1957), the women in the present study are a more heterogeneous population. The fact that almost two-fifths of the women believe they have at least one parent with a drinking problem supports the extremely high percentage of alcoholic women with parental problem drinking repeatedly reported in the literature. Also, these findings on parental alcoholism are quite similar to those recently reported by Mulford (1977), indicating that women alcoholics are more likely than men alcoholics to have an alcoholic father. Beckman (1975) earlier addressed the implications of such findings when she commented that this "may indicate the importance of cross-sex modeling as a factor in the etiology of alcoholism in women, or may suggest that alcoholism is causally related to some genetically inherited biochemical or metabolic imbalance" (p. 798). Other hypotheses will be suggested later.

A history of problem drinking in one or both parents varies by occupation, age, agency status of the subject, as well as the quantity of alcohol consumed. More than half of the professional women (53 percent) have a history of parental problem drinking as compared to a third (34 percent) of nonprofessional women ($p < .05$). Younger women, those under 30, are more likely to have parents with drinking problems (74 percent) than are older subjects ($p < .001$). Those women who are currently being treated as outpatients are least likely (28 percent) to have a history of parental problem drinking, while members of AA are most likely to have such a history (57 percent) ($p < .05$); inpatients with such a parental history fall between, with 41 percent reporting the presence of parental drinking problems. Finally, more than half of the subjects categorized as heavy or very heavy drinkers (those usually having at least 12 drinks) are likely to have a history of parental drinking problems than are women who drink less (28 percent), ($p < .05$).

In summary, almost two-fifths (39 percent) of the study women have a history of parents with a drinking problem and are more likely to have a father than a mother with such a problem. Professional women, women under age 30, AA women, and the heavier drinkers (at least 12 drinks usually) are most likely to have a history of parental drinking problems.

Siblings

The present study also examines the drinking background of siblings. In comparing siblings to the general population, Amark (1951) found that male siblings had considerably higher frequencies of alcoholism, but alcoholism among female siblings was not more frequently seen than alcoholism in the general population. In contrast, Lisansky (1957) stated that a higher percentage of female than male alcoholics have a sibling with a drinking problem; 24 percent of the women in her study reported problem drinking by a sibling, compared to only 9 percent of the men. When alcoholism among either male or female siblings is reported separately, alcoholism in brothers of alcoholic women ranges from 12 percent to 35 percent (Winokur and Clayton, 1968; Winokur et al., 1970) while alcoholism in sisters ranges from 7 percent (Mulford, 1977) to 18 percent (Schuckit, 1969).

Of the 98 subjects in the present study who have at least one sister, 13 percent have a sister who drinks the same or more. Of the 115 subjects who have at least one brother, 32 percent report at least one brother who drinks the same or more. Of the 129 subjects with at least one sibling, a total of 43 percent have at least one who drinks excessively; 59 percent of these siblings have never had help with their problem drinking.

These findings are consistent with those of Mulford (1977) and indicate that alcoholic women are more likely to have an alcoholic brother than an alcoholic sister, and that women alcoholics are more likely to have siblings, particularly a brother, who are alcoholic. When other relatives are included with parents and siblings, 61 percent of the subjects have at least one relative with a drinking problem.

Thus there is a fair amount of agreement when the present study women are compared with Mulford's study group, which is also a treated population. The greatest difference is the considerably higher percentage of women with sisters who have a drinking problem in the present study but otherwise they are quite similar to those of Schuckit's (1969) study group.

Sisters—a comparison group

Some two-thirds of the women in this study have a sister. In designing the study, it was planned to gather data on all sisters but to interview only those who did not have a drinking problem. It was anticipated such interviews would give insight into the differences in drinking patterns among women and would assist in guarding against false conclusions about the study subjects.

Lisansky (1957) had felt limited in her own study by a lack of knowledge "about the psychology of the normal non-alcoholic women with whom the alcoholic women must also eventually be compared." The data in this present study are the first to offer a description of women who are problem drinkers and their sisters.

It is not assumed that being reared in the same environment offers the same subjective experiences for two sisters; yet the choice of sisters seems superior to the alternative of matching women with drinking problems on certain preconceived variables to other women who do not have this problem. When studies concern themselves with etiology, as does this present study, it has been said that "siblings are preferable as comparison groups to non-related subjects. The use of siblings as controls minimizes the extent to which chance factors are responsible for differences between groups since siblings can be expected to resemble one another more closely" (Pollack and Gittelman, 1964). The comparison group of sisters will permit generalization about women alcoholics who have sisters. No comparison group is available in the present study for those who are an only child or who have brothers only.

It was anticipated that the withholding of permission by the study women to communicate with a sister for these interviews would be high and that refusals for participation by the sisters as research subjects would also result in a loss. It was also assumed that difficulties in locating sisters who do not have a drinking problem would further reduce the number of sisters available for interviews. The epidemiologist[1] who estimated that two of three women would have a sister was entirely correct since 98 living sisters were identified for 150 women and since 12 of the 98 sisters had a drinking problem, 86 sisters constitute the comparison group.

An estimate of a 50 percent interviewing loss because of refusals for such an interview, either by the study women or by their sisters, was made originally. As it turned out, this was quite accurate since 31 of the women were not willing to give permission to have their sisters interviewed and 14 sisters, in turn, refused to be interviewed. In addition, we were subsequently unable to locate seven sisters, and the data from one interview were incomplete. Thus data are available on 33 matched sisters. Where we could not interview sisters, minimal information was obtained from the 86 study women about their sisters who did not have a known drinking problem and constitutes the basis of reporting on all sisters.

The general questions we addressed in these interviews are: What differs in the life experiences of these sisters? Are there variables that can be identified in family or social experiences to account for the differences in drinking patterns between sisters?

The sister as well as the woman with a drinking problem were asked a series of open-ended questions to establish similarities and differences in a number of early and current life areas. Similar current descriptive background data were obtained, along with early family attitudes towards drinking, a description of the sister's own drinking practices, and her assessment of the reasons for the problem drinking of the study woman, if possible. The data obtained from the sisters were confined to the areas believed to be pertinent to establishing insights into etiology and the onset of problem drinking for the study women.

The hope of discerning critical differences between sisters through *retrospective* interviews is fraught with well-known research hazards. Yet, lacking longitudinal studies, a retrospective design is but one avenue of gaining a beginning understanding of critical phases of the development of alcoholism and should help to develop more precisely focused studies.

First, the data on all sisters, as obtained from the study subjects, will be discussed. We asked each woman to compare herself with her sister and then to characterize her response on a scale of "same, better, or worse" to a number of questions about their early family relationships and subsequent social and developmental events. In the first column of Table 6-1 is shown the percentage of study women responding "worse" to these questions. The first column gives the data for all of the 86 study women with non-alcoholic sisters; the second column, the responses of the 33 alcoholic women, each with a matched sister; the third column, those of their 33 non-alcoholic sisters. Finally, in the last column the responses of the matched sisters are compared.

A sign test was performed on each response. The sign test (see Appendix B) is similar to the one-sample binomial and determines if the positive and negative pairs are equal in the population under study. The sign test discards the response of "same" comparing only those responding better or worse. It was hypothesized that significantly more of the women would report having worse experiences than their sisters. The direction hypothesized for the sister data in the third column is for significantly fewer of the sisters to respond worse. Thus a one-tailed test is used since the direction is predicted for this data. Only those items that are significantly different in the direction predicted are shown with an asterisk.

In the first column, five questions are shown as reaching a statistically significant difference for all 86 alcoholic women: having, at present, fewer friends and worse financial security, mental health, emotional security, and satisfaction in marriage. All questions relate to the present.

TABLE 6-1 *All Women With Sisters and the Matched Sisters Perceiving a Number of Life Situations As Worse When Comparing Self With Sister: Percentage Distribution*

	PERCENTAGE WORSE[a]			
	All study women: with non-alcoholic sisters (N=86)	Matched sisters (N=33)		P Comparing Matched Sisters
		Study women	Sisters	
Early family relationships				
Father	45	47	*26	NS
Mother	58	69	*21	NS
Brother	27	22	42	NS
Sisters	25	40	* 0	NS
Only sister	41	43	57	NS
Social life				
Teenager	55	67	37	NS
Young adult	43	52	*26	NS
Specifics of social development				
Fewer friends as a child	43	58	59	NS
Fewer friends as a young adult	44	50	47	NS
School				
Grades	43	38	58	NS
Present				
Job satisfaction	42	69	* 0	.01
Friends (fewer)	*68	*76	*11	.05
Financial security	*73	*84	* 5	.001
Health				
Physical	63	*75	*10	NS
Mental health	*90	*95	* 0	.01
Emotional security	*85	*88	* 0	.001
Marriage and children				
Satisfaction (in marriage)	*71	*92	* 0	.05
Relations with children	68	0	* 0	NS

* Sign test: $p<.05$ (1 tail)
[a] The reader will note that similar percentages are not always statistically significant; this is accounted for by differential bases; also the numbers are small in some instances.

When the same sign test is applied to the subgroup of alcoholic women whose matched sister was interviewed (second column), one additional significant difference emerges. A somewhat higher proportion view their physical health as significantly worse; the other significant relationships reported by the 86 women persist. Thus, the 33 study women whose sisters were interviewed do not differ appreciably from all the women with non-alcoholic sisters on these questions.

Many of the questions for the matched non-alcoholic sisters have statistically significant results as shown in the third column. This is accounted for by the relatively fewer instances in which the sisters reported themselves as worse. Thus, when they compared themselves to their alcoholic sisters, the sisters perceive themselves as better in those areas shown to have statistically significant differences. This is true for their relationships with both mothers, fathers, and sisters; their social life as young adults; and certainly in every aspect of their present life. Thus, the individual analysis of the independent responses of the matched sisters shown in the second and third columns indicates agreement when both sisters give responses that are significant in differing direction; for example, a higher proportion of alcoholic women consider themselves "worse" when asked about friends at present while the sisters are more likely to describe themselves as better. Both are significant.

There tends, then, to be agreement on many items between the sisters, and this is best reflected in the last column comparing the response of the matched sisters. The last column, however, adds an additional dimension to understanding these data. A significant difference in the last column indicates agreement between the matched sisters. The perceptions of the sisters imply agreement for the present but not for the past. The lack of statistical significance indicates there is no general agreement that the women are more or less worse in these areas than their sisters. Thus the statistical significance shows they agree that the alcoholic woman's job, friends, financial security, mental health, emotional security, and satisfaction in marriage are worse and the sister's are better.

At times fewer of the non-alcoholic sisters characterize their early relationships as worse than those of their alcoholic sisters, but the numbers are not sufficiently different for statistical significance to be achieved. For example, more of the women recall early family relationships with their mothers as worse, but the small sample size prevents the difference from reaching statistically significant results. Since more of the alcoholic women generally recall their early relationships as worse, this may be a clue for future researchers who are able to study a larger sample with more refined measures prospectively. Sibling relationships and grades are in the opposite direction of that predicted for the women but again fail to reach significance and cannot be given too much emphasis from this one study. Yet more of the alcoholic women seem to have functioned well in school as shown in the question on grades. They may, indeed, have done better in school and achieved at a higher level, but the caution on sample size again applies.

The following material relates to the 33 matched sister pairs—the 33 alcoholic women and their 33 non-alcoholic sisters—who are asked similar questions about their early and present life.

AGE

As a group, the sisters are almost exactly the same age when interviewed as that of the study women; although reporting a slightly younger average age at which drinking began, this more advanced age is not statistically different. Asked, too, "when" drinking became a problem for the women, the sisters report somewhat *fewer* years elapsing since the start of problem drinking; this too, is not a statistically significant difference but generally is in the direction of supporting the woman's self-report. Since the sisters report somewhat fewer years, it also tends to reinforce the perception of the study women being able to mask their drinking problem from others (Table 6–2).

TABLE 6–2 *Matched Sisters: Present Age, Age Started Drinking, and Years Elapsing Since Drinking Problems Began*

	NUMBER OF YEARS		
MATCHED SISTERS	Women N=33	Sisters N=33	P
Present age	38.8	38.7	NS
First started drinking	19.6	17.9	NS
Drinking problem began for study women (years prior)	12.3	10.3	NS

EARLY LIFE EXPERIENCES

Most of the paired sisters lived with both parents growing up. The exceptions were few, but when they existed, they were less favorable for the alcoholic women. For example, five of the study women but only one non-alcoholic sister lived with other relatives. Almost half of the study women (48 percent) recall their early years as unhappy whereas only 12 percent of the sisters had such a recollection ($p < .01$). Fifty-two percent of the study women believe they were treated equally by their parents as compared to 64 percent of the sisters, but this is not a significant difference.

SISTERS' PERCEPTIONS OF PARENTAL DRINKING

The pair matched sisters perceive the existence of parental drinking and the existence of any parental drunkenness very much the same. No significant differences emerged on the series of questions asked about the history of family drinking.

SISTERS: THOSE MARRIED AND THOSE LIVING ALONE

There is no significant difference between the proportion of matched sisters who ever married. As expected, a difference does appear in the proportion who are currently married, and it is a significant difference ($p < .01$). While 70 percent of the study women are not currently married, the very same percentage of their sisters are married. This, in turn, fits with the difference in the study women's living situations as compared with those of their sisters since more of the study women are currently likely to be living alone.

FRIENDS

There are a number of differences that emerge between the matched sisters on their current social interactions. The limited social activities of the study women were discussed earlier as they related to their drinking problem. When the sisters are compared, the study women are significantly less likely to visit friends, to have friends visit, or to go out with friends than are their sisters ($p < .05$). Using each of these three items to form an index of social relationships, a sum of these social interactions was obtained. This score shows a significant difference between the paired sisters: While the study women obtain a mean score of 1.9 on this index of social relations, their sisters score close to the maximum (2.7) on a scale of zero to three. As expected, too, the standard deviation for the women is relatively wide (1.2), whereas it varies little for the sisters (.585) reflecting the greater consistency among the sisters in their social relations.

EMOTIONAL HEALTH

Using the 22 items Langner (1962) described to measure emotional health, the matched sisters show a significant difference on the sum of the scores. A score of 7 or more denotes psychiatric impairment. (This scale was discussed earlier in Chapter 4.) The matched women with a drinking problem have an average score of 10.2 while the sisters have a score of 4.2. Such a difference is, of course, statistically significant ($p < .001$). As shown in Table 6–3, 73 percent of the women with a drinking problem are impaired (with a score of 7 or more) on entering treatment as compared to only 18 percent of their non-alcoholic sisters.

Each of the 22 items was reviewed individually, and the McNemar test of significance (Appendix B) was used to assess if there was any area in which the matched sisters might be expressing differing emotional distress. While 15 items showed significant differences, all favored the non-alcoholic sisters, who proved to have *fewer* of these symptoms. Thus, more of the alcoholic women had a poor appetite, periods of restlessness, trouble with sleeping, poor memory, and so on. In no instance did the sisters have a consistently higher percentage of symptoms on these individual items.

TABLE 6–3 *Emotional Health Symptom Score: Percentage Distribution for Women and Their Matched Sister*

SYMPTOM SCORE	WOMEN[a] (N=33)	SISTER (N=33)
Well (0–3)	6	39
Mild (4)	6	18
Moderate (5–6)	15	24
Impaired (7 or more)	73	18
(Mean)	(10.2)	(4.2)

[a] Symptom score as they entered treatment for alcoholism.
t value 8.07, $p < .001$

Of some interest, however, are those items that reflected no difference between the sisters. These were responses to questions about worrying, their heart beating hard, shortness of breath, nervousness, fainting spells, acid stomach, and fullness in their head or nose. "Worrying" and "nervousness," both indicators of anxiety, ranked high in the symptomatology; 91 percent and 64 percent for the women, respectively, and 76 percent and 71 percent for the sisters.

SLEEPING PILLS AND TRANQUILIZERS

Sleeping pills were not in extensive use among the matched sisters and, in fact, their use is lower than expected. Only about one-third of the study women ever took sleeping pills, and their matched sisters were very close in usage with 27 percent reporting a lifetime use. This is not a statistically significant difference between the sisters. The use of tranquilizers was prevalent among the matched sisters. Almost four-fifths of the women take tranquilizers, most of them currently, in contrast to just under half of their sisters also using tranquilizers. This is a significant difference ($< .05$). These figures may be a good approximation of the high usage of tranquilizers by women and the significantly higher and dangerous usage by alcoholic women.

In Chapter 3 we described the frequency, duration of other drug taking, and data on drinking with other drug use in addition to current usage, defined as usage in the last three months. Current usage of any drug by the non-alcoholic sisters is relatively low. None acknowledge recent heroin use, but one sister continues on a maintenance dose of methadone. Current usage falls to a third or half for lifetime use of sleeping pills, tranquilizers, and marijuana for both the women and matched sisters. With the exception of the one sister currently on methadone, the data suggest that the non-alcoholic sisters, as a group, have not been dependent on other drugs. There is support for this in their own report of behavior under stress. When asked if they take a pill to calm them down or cheer them up "a lot, sometimes, or never," 73 percent said "never." An even higher percentage (82 percent) said they never drink when nervous or depressed.

DRINKING BY THE NON-ALCOHOLIC SISTERS

Most of the non-alcoholic sisters drink, but at the time of the interview, eight (24 percent) did not and three of these eight never did drink. Only two of the sisters drink daily, and another two drink nearly every day. Most characterized their drinking as fairly light, selecting from among the following descriptions of drinking: "fairly light," "fairly heavy," "heavy." In contrast, 26 of the 33 sisters thought the study women were "heavy" drinkers.

SOCIAL-ESCAPIST REASONS FOR DRINKING

In Chapter 3, when describing the study women's patterns of drinking, the social-escapist index used to assess their reasons for drinking was discussed. Most of the alcoholic women gave reasons identified as escapist, and it was noted that such reasons have been found to be good predictors of current or future problems with alcohol. In Table 6–4, the response of the matched sisters is compared with that of other heavy- and light-drinking women who have been asked these same questions about their reasons for drinking (Cahalan, Cisin, and Crossley, 1969, p. 167). The non-alcoholic sisters compare favorably to other light-drinking women; on the average they gave less than one (.76)

TABLE 6–4 *Reasons for Drinking: Percentage Distribution of Study Women Compared with Matched Sisters and Heavy- and Light-Drinking American Women*

ESCAPIST-SOCIAL AND OTHER REASONS FOR DRINKING	STUDY WOMEN (N=33)	HEAVY-DRINKING AMERICAN WOMEN (N=72)	NON-ALCOHOLIC SISTERS (N=33)	LIGHT-DRINKING AMERICAN WOMEN (N=442)
Help to relax (E)	91	76	30	40
Sociable (S)	39	82	52	70
Like taste (O)	39	71	42	44
People I know drink (S)	39	55	27	33
To forget everything (E)	94	22	6	6
Celebrate special occasions (S)	55	83	70	75
Helps forget worries (E)	97	43	3	12
Improves appetite (O)	27	31	12	30
Polite thing to do (S)	12	60	36	59
Helps cheer up (E)	76	53	24	20
Need when tense (E)	91	51	12	17

KEY: (E) Escapist reasons for drinking
(S) Social reasons for drinking
(O) Other—enjoyment oriented

escapist reason for drinking. They were considerably more likely to offer a social reason for drinking (1.85). The alcoholic women, in contrast, exceeded the heavy-drinking American women on the proportion giving escapist reasons and were found to have between four and five escapist reasons (on the average, 4.49). As noted for the total study group, the matched study women were less likely to give social reasons for drinking (1.46), and this is slightly less than the average social score (1.85) of the sisters. While the difference between the sisters on escapist reasons is statistically significant ($p < .001$), the difference on social reasons is not ($p < .239$).

The sisters view each other
THE STUDY WOMAN'S VIEW—WHY HER SISTER DRINKS LESS

Hoping to pick up some clues to etiology, we asked the study woman why she thought her sister drank less. A number of women (10) pointed to two aspects of alcohol which differed for their sisters: taste and effect. Either they believed their sisters did not like the taste, they did not like the effect, or both were operating.

I think they just don't like it—they don't like the taste. They did try it but don't like what it does to them. They got obnoxious, but not as bad as me.

She simply does not like it, or what it does for her.

She doesn't want to. She doesn't care for it.

There were several other women (six) who could point to their sisters having experienced more of the "good life."

She is happy, content, and has everything she wants.

Maybe she just doesn't have a problem. She is married to a man who drinks the same as she does. Maybe because she is not alone and is too busy.

She got involved with nice people. She graduated from college and is now a teacher. She is also married and has a very good life.

She figures she is better than I am. She has family and money. I'm what you call an outcast.

A number of women thought there might be differences that could be accounted for by a chemical imbalance, even a difference in self-esteem, or coping ability. Also, some simply said they did not know.

I don't know. My mother was an alcoholic and so is my father and brother. We all seem susceptible to alcohol. My brother who died also drank a lot.

THE SISTERS' VIEW—WHY THE STUDY WOMAN DRINKS MORE

There were relatively few sisters who could not account for the women having a drinking problem. In fact, they offered an almost infinite number of reasons beginning with a lack of confidence, or differences in coping ability, but most frequently they mentioned current problems in a marriage or other relationships, and even the influence of a drinking husband.

She married a drinking husband. Lots of times she said she got drunk because he did, which was a poor excuse.

She had marriage problems and problems with her children that I didn't have. My sister never gives vent to her emotions, her husband wouldn't allow it.

She has a husband who does not understand her and uses his fists on her.

SISTERS' PERCEPTIONS OF DRINKING WOMEN

We explored with the non-alcoholic sisters their own perceptions of drinking women. There was convergence between the matched sisters in their responses to questions on whether it was worse for a woman or man to drink too much. More than half agreed it was worse for a woman. They also agreed that women were more sexually available when drinking. Differences between the sisters emerged when rejection was discussed. While very high proportions of the non-alcoholic sisters believe drinking women are more rejected socially than men (70 percent), more of the alcoholic women (94 percent) believe this to be so ($p < .05$). This perception of self must, indeed, play a part in why fewer women appear in treatment.

THE SISTERS AS MOTHERS—OUTCOME FOR THE CHILDREN

Most of the matched sisters became mothers; 13 of the study women and 9 of their sisters did not. While we have a fairly similar number of matched sisters who had children, the number becomes smaller when describing the children; there are only 15 pairs of matched sisters with children. As mothers, one major difference is apparent: The alcoholic study woman is less likely to be the primary caretaker, and this is close to a significant difference ($p < .06$). Separations are also more likely for the children of the alcoholic women ($p < .05$): Forty percent reported separations as compared to 25 percent for the children of the non-alcoholic sisters. Charges of negligence by the court are rare, and there is no significant difference between the sisters.

Of considerable interest is the information gleaned as it relates to the development of the children. None of these differences, however, reach the level of significance set for the study. *Fewer* of the alcoholic women reported learning problems for their children, and there were fewer school absences. There was a similar likelihood of the school calling to discuss their children, but no difference is found among the children with poor grades. Somewhat fewer of the alcoholic study women reported outside social activities for their children, 65 percent for their children as compared to 83 percent for their sisters' children. Again, this is not a significant difference. The direction of the difference each time is for the study women to report their children having few friends, or the children bringing few friends home.

The relationship between the children and both their parents is more likely to be defined as poor—15 percent for the children of the alcoholic women as compared to 4 percent for the sisters. There is also a somewhat greater likelihood for a poor relationship with fathers—25 percent are poor, as described by the study women, while only 4 percent of the sisters reported a poor paternal relationship.

Etiology of alcoholism

There is strong reason to believe that societal norms for women very much influence not only who drinks, but the quantity consumed. In addition, as discussed in Chapter 4, Jones and Jones (1976a,b) point to a decidedly different experience for women who drink than for men. In contrast to men, it may be that for women differing physiological responses, differing cultural norms, and differing socialization experiences all form powerful nonspecific factors influencing the effects of alcohol on them (Rickels, 1968).

The present study obviously was an opportunity to explore some of the psychosocial explanations about the development of alcoholism in women. In their writings on the origins of alcoholism, McCord and McCord (1960) trace the Cambridge-Somerville boys into adulthood and compare the "minority who became alcoholic with the majority."

Developing a series of post-hoc hypotheses, they tested them on the available data. They conclude that:

The "predisposition" to alcoholism is established rather early in life, through the person's intimate experiences within his family. This theory is necessarily a speculative one, but it is supported not only by the longitudinal data, but indirectly by such well-established facts as the male-female difference in rates of alcoholism.

In an earlier section, titled "Some Speculations on Female Alcoholism," these same authors state:

Whereas male alcoholism is "favored" by heightened dependency needs that conflict with expectations entailed in the masculine role, this conflict does not occur as frequently for the female in America. Perhaps as the woman's role becomes increasingly "masculine," the female potential alcoholic will find non-alcoholic satisfactions less available.

The female alcoholic is more likely to have a background of role confusion than one of dependency conflict. Her inability to accept her role could be the result of parental expectations that conflict with the cultural delineation of the female role, of an early environment that "punished" the girl's attempts to perform female role activities, or of a *female* model whose behavior is markedly different from "the norm."

We explored these theoretical formulations on role confusion as a possible precursor of alcoholism in women and used them to guide the development of a series of hypotheses that we examined by comparing the responses of the matched sisters. Through a series of open-ended questions, we assessed such role confusion for its existence prior to adulthood.

ROLE CONFUSION

If there is any support for "role confusion" as the basis for alcoholism in women, it was hypothesized that significantly more of the study women, in contrast to their non-alcoholic sisters, would report experiencing such role confusion.

The following items were considered to be indicators of role confusion:

1. Parental expectations conflicting with the female role
2. Parental punishment for the female role
3. Role models that called for behavior different from approved parental norms

It was hypothesized that the alcoholic woman would have a significantly higher score than her sister on those items denoting role confusion.

These areas were then translated into the following specific questions:

Did either of your parents ever expect you to do things that were different from what other girls did?

Were you ever punished by either of your parents for any activity that girls usually enjoy doing?

Were there any things you did growing up that you might have enjoyed, but your parents either did not approve or showed no interest?

Is there anyone you looked up to when you were growing up? Did your family approve?

More of the study women believe their parents expected them to do things that were different from what other girls did, 52 percent as compared to 33 percent of the sisters. This is not, however, a significant difference ($p < .181$). There is no difference either in the proportion reporting punishment for what girls usually do. A substantial and significant difference does obtain in lack of parental approval or interest. Approximately two-thirds of the study women (67 percent) reported experiencing parental disapproval or lack of interest in what they enjoyed doing whereas less than two-fifths of the sisters found this to be true. This is both a meaningful and significant difference ($p < .01$). As to their role model and parental approval, there is also

TABLE 6-5 *Average Score For Study Women and Non-Alcoholic Sisters on Four Indicators of Role Confusion*

	MEAN	t VALUES	P
Study women	2.0	1.63	<.056
Non-alcoholic sister	1.6		

no difference between the sisters. Thus only one of the four questions yields statistically significant results.

We then proceeded to sum the four responses. The score is shown in Table 6-5.

The more conservative Wilcoxin matched-pairs signed-ranks test for nonparametric data was also applied, and using a one-tailed test, a probability of $p < .07$ was obtained. Obviously neither test indicates significant differences at the level set but is close to a significant difference.

By using such gross indicators of role confusion one may cautiously conclude that there is some tenuous evidence to support the hypothesis of women problem drinkers perceiving their parents differently than their non-alcoholic sisters. Whether or not this difference in perception lends support to a conclusion of role confusion, which may be causally related in turn to alcoholism, is moot. What is more apparent is that the women recall their parents as "less approving." Clearly more refined measures of role confusion must be applied if unequivocal results are to be achieved.

SEX-ROLE IDENTIFICATION

The area of sex-role identification of the matched sisters was also explored. Anderson (1976)[2] replicated an earlier study by Wilsnack (1973). The availability of sisters for comparison in this replication was seen as offering a more rigorous control group than had been possible in the earlier study. Contrary to the findings of Wilsnack that alcoholic women are more masculine than non-alcoholic women in unconscious identification, we found in the present study no significant differences between the alcoholic women and their non-alcoholic sisters on any of the measures utilized. In fact, the study women and their sisters were more masculine in unconscious identification than the female norm, but the control sisters seemed to reflect greater consistency between actual behavior and attitudes than did the alcoholic women.

Anderson also built on the work of M. C. Jones (1971), who had earlier identified a cluster of personality traits characterizing the alcoholic woman as an adolescent from a longitudinal study. Anderson's own work attempted to determine whether, in retrospect, alcoholic women describe themselves as manifesting significantly different traits during adolescence from those of their non-alcoholic sisters. Using 14 personality traits drawn primarily from the Jones study, two significant differences emerged. More of the alcoholic women described themselves as withdrawn and full of doubt during adolescence. Yet the matched sisters did not perceive themselves as different when asked to describe each other during adolescence.

The concept of ultrafemininity was also examined since Jones had reported alcoholic women as typically ultrafeminine during adolescence. The group we analyzed in the present study group does not support the Jones finding. In fact, the non-alcoholic sister controls perceived themselves to be significantly more ultrafeminine as adolescents than did the alcoholic women.

Eight of the traits that discriminated between the sisters predicted accurately the likelihood of alcoholism for 83 percent of the women and non-alcoholism in 73 percent of the controls. Anderson's research contributes substantially to the dialogue on sex-role identification of alcoholic women. She concludes that while the alcoholic woman and her sister as adults are both more masculine than the female norm in sex-role style and unconscious identification, the pre-alcoholic adolescent perceives herself as more competent and thinks of herself as lacking the ultrafeminine traits of her sister. Anderson speculates that *some* girls who later become problem drinkers learn in early adolescence that their competence is incompatible with femininity as defined by society. Anderson thinks this realization may be reflected in the self-doubt, withdrawal, and moodiness reported by them but not by their non-alcoholic sisters.

Conclusions

This wide-ranging chapter on the family takes both a similar and different path from prior studies. The similarities relate to the detailed history of family problem drinking, which has been shown to be quite high and supports other studies in alcoholism. Parental drunkenness is also noted to be quite high for these study women. The variations in parental drunkenness by the woman's age probably portends poorly for future generations and drinking by women. For example, while 3 percent of the women over 50 observed their mother drunk, 55 percent of those under 30 reported such an occurrence.

The difference in the present study design from other descriptive studies is the inclusion of non-alcoholic sisters as a comparison group. It was anticipated that the most positive contribution of this approach would be to guard against false conclusions in addition to providing leads for others to pursue more rigorously. Exploring the experiences of the alcoholic women in the present and past as compared with those of their sisters yields a clearer direction for future work in this area.

We have tried to determine what differed in the life experiences of the matched sisters and to identify variables that could account for the alcoholism of the study women. Do the sisters and study women perceive their life experiences as essentially the same, or does either group perceive significant differences between them? To overcome extraneous differences we used non-alcoholic sisters closest in age to the study women as controls. Some 86 study women were identified as having sisters who met this criteria but only 33 could be interviewed, primarily because of the high number of study women who withheld permission. The results must be interpreted with caution because of the smaller numbers interviewed and of the retrospective nature of the data.

Differences are reported by the non-alcoholic sisters in their early family relationships, which they consistently recall as better than do the alcoholic women. Also, other early life differences were possibly more negative for the study women, such as living with relatives. There is a hint, too, that the study women experienced their parents differently, and felt less accepted than their non-alcoholic sisters. Based on studying the same matched sisters, Anderson's exploration of sex-role identification may support such an interpretation since she finds that *some* alcoholic women "learn in early adolescence that their competence is incompatible with femininity as defined by society," (that is, parents representing society) and this results in self-doubt, and so on. Obviously, what seems to happen to the alcoholic women in their adult life must be viewed in combination with these earlier experiences. Many are less likely to form satisfactory relationships—this is best reflected in the data on those who married. In contrast the matched non-alcoholic sisters are more likely to have a satisfactory marriage, or at least they remain in a marriage.

These data point to the etiology of alcoholism in women as due to a combination of factors:

1. Many have an early exposure to parental problems with drinking. Yet nearly two-fifths do not have any relative with a drinking problem.
2. When compared with their matched sisters, the study women seem to have experienced during early life less acceptance and approval by parents than did their sisters.
3. In adult life, the study women do not find satisfying relationships, especially as reflected in their marriages. The cause of failures in many of the marriages are not attributed directly by the women to their drinking.

More of the study women as compared to their matched sisters recall an unhappy childhood. In adulthood, they continue to report unhappy and less satisfying experiences. In contrast, the sisters have more stable supportive experiences. They are also less likely to have married men who drink or men who have a drinking problem. Thus, the non-alcoholic sisters experience relatively benign adult relationships.

If psychosocial development is sufficient to account for the alcoholism of the study women, then the total life experience, beginning with early family relationships, is a critical area. At the same time, the function of the more benign adult experiences of the matched sisters must be examined carefully in assessing their lack of a drinking problem. Indeed, the psychosocial aspects of the development of alcoholism point to the need for longitudinal studies rather than for reliance on retrospective data.

Notes
1. Ray Glazier then on the staff of the Research Department of the Community Council of Greater New York.
2. This portion of the study of sisters on sex-role identification was carried out by Sandra C. Anderson and constituted her doctoral dissertation (1976).

7
Outcome of Treatment

Summary of findings

As the women enter treatment, the treatment settings emphasize the physical consequences of alcoholism. Most receive vitamins or tranquilizers; antabuse is taken by a few.

Individual and group treatment is also heavily emphasized. Alcoholism counselors and social workers play a major role in such treatment. Alcoholics Anonymous (AA) seems to be an integral component of most treatment programs. Family counseling plays a relatively minor role.

A substantial proportion of the study women (41 percent) had not had a drink since the first research interview, which had occurred, on the average, 13 months earlier; and an additional 12 percent had had a drink only on a rare occasion.

Seventy-one percent of the women had not been drinking in the month prior to the follow-up research interview, and for more than half it was 6 months since their last drink.

Professional women, women in the highest socioeconomic group, and white women are significantly more likely to be totally abstinent.

A significantly different drinking outcome by the type of entry agency is accounted for by the low percentage of abstainers among the original outpatients and the high percentage of abstainers among those entering the research study from Alcoholics Anonymous.

Because of the large number of women who at some point attended AA, the effect of AA on treatment results is examined and found to have minimal impact on abstinence if AA is the only form of help.

Those women whose drinking lessened at the follow-up all show a dramatic decrease in their emotional health score, reflecting a decrease in symptomatology. Abstention, however, seems to be the overriding variable to explain this result.

The drinking outcome does not show any difference by the women's employment.

An appreciable number of women have been treated for their drinking, and some have obviously been treated for considerable periods of time prior to their current treatment. Having experienced such prior treatment proves to be a meaningful variable in current abstinence.

When help for a specific problem or illness is sought, how should the results of such treatment be measured? One measure used frequently in alcohol studies is the complete alleviation of drinking, or at least a reasonable lapse of time since the person last drank. Most professional helpers and researchers also usually look for changes in other areas of behavior and functioning, such as improved health, job performance, and interpersonal relations.

Some researchers and therapists look for a return to moderation in drinking. A reduction in the dosage of alcohol has been used in several studies as a measure of improvement (Gerard and Sanger, 1966; Armor, Polich, and Stambul, 1976). This concept of controlled or normal drinking has entered the alcoholism literature to denote those individuals whose drinking has lessened or returned to a more "normal" range and where the drinking creates less problems in a variety of life spheres.

Several dimensions studied in the initial and follow-up interviews will be described here. Focus will be on changes, if any, in drinking, employment, and emotional health and will be discussed in relation to the background variables used throughout the study. First, let us consider the treatment settings and the treatment received.

The treatment settings

The settings for treatment are almost as varied as the women themselves. The time period in which we will describe the hospitals, clinics, residential programs, and Alcoholics Anonymous is the period when the women entered these treatment programs. Some of the treatment settings may have changed considerably since that time, either because their services have expanded or even new philosophies of treatment are now in existence. It is known that one state facility in the suburban locale is now closed.

It is usually quite difficult to capture the unique ingredients that individuals experience in treatment. The broad classification of inpatient and outpatient services itself denotes an extremely wide range of treatment. The inpatient service may actually be a few days of hospitalization to allow for detoxification which is simply defined as the "recovery from the effects of alcohol in the organism" (Keller and McCormick, 1968, p. 73). By contrast, it can be several weeks to several months of a hospital stay, or even a residential program, that may also emphasize initially the withdrawal of alcohol and the need to safeguard against the harmful effects of withdrawal. The more prolonged period of treatment beyond withdrawal and detoxification is usually devoted to individual or group treatment, to education about alcohol, and also quite typically to attendance at AA meetings. But many women may seek help at clinics, often in hospitals, which may not involve more than a weekly appointment as outpatients. There is the same variability in Alcoholics Anonymous (AA) groups, although all groups have adopted the same philosophy based on acknowledging that drinking is no longer under the individual's control. Many of the hospitals and clinics incorporate meetings of AA groups in their own programs which offer the possibility of a support system when individuals return to their community and to other groups.

Each of the settings from which the women were selected will be described, followed by comments by some of the women about their experiences. We have given anonymity to all the clinics and hospitals by using only alphabetic designations for each. The urban metropolitan clinics and hospitals numbered seven as did the suburban clinics and hospitals. Thus a total of 14 treatment settings are described. Some of the hospitals offered 3 to 5 days of detoxification and then made referrals elsewhere; or the hospitals encouraged a longer stay but also referred elsewhere on discharge; or hospitals provided the relatively brief or longer period of inpatient care, followed by treatment as an outpatient. Outpatient services usually involved groups or individual treatment on a once weekly basis. Most settings encouraged continued attendance at AA.

SUBURBAN PROGRAMS

Residence A. An inpatient residential unit in a beautiful rural setting. A series of lodgelike units house the students. The environment is described as "structured and nonpermissive." There is heavy emphasis on educational lectures about alcohol, which may include guest lecturers, tapes, and films. Family therapy is also available. Attendance at AA meetings is a major component of the program.

Hospital B. This public hospital was just beginning its alcoholism program on an inpatient and outpatient basis. Located in one of the wealthiest counties of the state, it was offering medical education, psychiatric evaluation, psychological testing, counseling, and occupational therapy. Alcoholics Anonymous held regular meetings at the hospital. Family counseling, individual therapy, and group therapy were available. The staff consisted of professional persons under the direction of a psychiatrist.

Hospital C. As a private inpatient psychiatric service this hospital had a large separate alcoholism unit of almost 75 patients who shared semiprivate rooms. Patients received both medical and psychiatric consultation. This program, too, works closely with AA and a large number of meetings are available both at the hospital and in the local community. Family participation in the treatment process is strongly urged. Patients usually stayed several weeks. Continued treatment most usually occurred in a patient's own community.

Hospital D. A general voluntary hospital located in a small suburban community, it offers outpatient treatment only. Individual counseling by social workers was most characteristic of this clinic; vocational counseling and AA affiliation were also encouraged.

Hospital E. As a state facility, this program offered short-term hospitalization initially for detoxification and then living in a large cottage on the grounds as a transitional residence emphasizing group life and interaction. Individual as well as group therapy are available from the medical and social work staff.

Hospital F. This new alcoholism service at a voluntary hospital in an essentially middle- and upper-class suburban community served inpatients who were identified as having alcohol problems by their private physicians. Counseling by the staff of the alcoholism program was given while patients were in the hospital. An outpatient counseling service was also available to patients when they were discharged. The patient's private physician was pivotal in this program.

Hospital G. This was a fairly well-established alcoholism treatment center located in a parklike setting at a voluntary hospital. Both inpatient and outpatient services were available. Individual and group treatments were provided.

URBAN PROGRAMS

Clinic A. This outpatient service offered extensive and varied programs that gave major emphasis to group therapy. In addition, individual therapy, family counseling, marital therapy, and vocational counseling were also available. It was part of a health center that also provided inpatient detoxification service for alcoholics (see Hospital C).

Hospital B. This large voluntary hospital emphasized detoxification with referral to the patient's home community for continued care.

Hospital C. Similar to urban Hospital B in its emphasis on detoxification, this voluntary hospital also had an affiliation with an outpatient service to which patients could be referred upon discharge.

Hospital D. This private hospital had a number of beds for detoxification. In addition to general medical treatment, it offered alcohol education. It did not offer any outpatient care.

Hospital and Clinic E. Located in an inner city area, this general hospital had a number of beds for medical detoxification. A medical and psychiatric examination was required on admission. The comprehensive service provided individual and group therapy, family counseling, marital therapy, AA meetings, and basic remedial education. Chemotherapy was also available. Patients could continue to receive treatment in the outpatient clinic on discharge from the hospital.

Hospital and Clinic F. Located in a busy midtown area, this hospital, too, had a comprehensive program that enabled patients to move from the inpatient service to continued care in the outpatient service.

Residence G. Affiliated with the hospital and clinic just described this residential facility was geographically separate. It, too, offered a range of services in a therapeutic environment; its orientation is that of Alcoholics Anonymous. The usual length of stay for patients was 28 days.

STUDY WOMEN'S EVALUATIONS OF TREATMENT SETTINGS

Following are the comments of some of the women as they recalled their experience on entry to the treatment setting. These are not given in any particular order and are included to represent a cross-section of experiences as recalled by the women almost one year after they began their treatment.

It is something I needed very badly. They give you a new outlook on alcohol and life, and I have a great respect for alcohol now. I know I can't drink hard liquor. I feel great that I can accept not having a drink. I wish it weren't so far away. I'd like to stop in once in awhile. . . .

They really drill it into you what damage alcohol can do to you. I never realized how bad it really was . . .

The lectures were enlightening; the educational program was very good and a necessary step to stop drinking. You couldn't stop drinking without that help. A fun place; I enjoyed it.

It was the best hospital. Unfortunately, after I left although I followed up with AA meetings it could not sustain me.

I knew I was an alcoholic and couldn't drink when I went there. They reinforced that.

I didn't think I was an alcoholic until I went there. My life has certainly changed . . . I go to four or five AA meetings a week . . . My life is happy with my husband and children, which I wouldn't have had . . . I have found that I could be happy without drugs and alcohol.

They taught about the disease. I learned not to be ashamed; it is a physical problem.

I learned about the disease of alcoholism. I learned to live a life without alcohol and drugs. The discipline was strict and at times more severe than you would have liked.

It has helped me to relate to other people through the group participation; by identifying with others, the problems of drinking were shared. I have been able to take on speaking engagements for AA groups.

I tried treatment, but it was no good. It was only seven days. After being alcoholic for sixteen years, seven days doesn't even matter.

After those seven days they discharged me, and I felt I could make it by myself. They were giving me medication for sleep, pain, and so on.

There were a lot of meetings. It is rotten making you tell your life. I lost interest.

They got me interested in AA. They showed me it was the only thing that was going to save me.

The group discussions were helpful. I had someone to talk to, someone who understood. I had very good medical treatment.

I am living, not just existing. My sobriety is the most important thing for me . . .

While these comments were made in response to asking the woman's view of her earlier treatment, they tend to reveal her own estimate of its success as well as her perception of the treatment itself.

The agency[1]

The data from the agencies gives a good sense of the beginning of treatment, the goals for the patients, and the background of the staff involved in the treatment. The treatment agencies' report of their activity is briefly described.

For most patients there is emphasis on the physical consequences of their illness as reflected in the large numbers seen by physicians and nurses, 69 percent and 64 percent, respectively. The prominence of alcoholism counselors in treatment programs is amply demonstrated by the large number of women seen by such counselors (63 percent). Social workers are also a major component in the treatment efforts, with 55 percent of the women being seen by social workers. Fewer psychiatrists (40 percent) and even fewer psychologists (29 percent) are involved in treatment programs.

Most of the women were given vitamins (66 percent) or tranquilizers (41 percent), whereas antabuse, an alcohol antagonist, was prescribed for relatively few (only 13 percent). There is heavy emphasis on individual treatment (85 percent) and group treatment (76 percent). Alcoholics Anonymous also play a major part at most of the settings, with 69 percent of the women participating in AA at the treatment agencies. Educational meetings are quite prevalent (52 percent). Family counseling or participation seems to play a relatively minor role in treatment at these settings (23 percent).

The staff's goal in treatment is abstinence for almost all (94 percent), but only 40 percent of the women are considered to have a good to excellent chance of reaching that goal, 34 percent a fair chance, with 25 percent viewed as having a poor to very poor chance.

Outcome of treatment: Effects on drinking

Of the 116 women interviewed at the time of the follow-up interview, 71 percent had not been drinking during the prior month. (The sample loss is discussed in Appendix A.) For more than half it has been more than 6 months since they had a drink. Those who do drink continue to be daily or almost daily drinkers with slightly less than a third defining themselves as binge drinkers.[2]

A substantial proportion (41 percent) had not had a drink since the first research interview, which occurred on the average 13 months earlier, and an additional eighth (12 percent) had a drink only on a rare occasion.[3] This outcome accounts for slightly more than half of the women interviewed, (53 percent) and can be viewed as a startling good result. Even without the inclusion of those drinking on a "rare occa-

Outcome of Treatment

sion" it still remains a most impressive 41 percent of the women who abstained from drinking after an average of 13 months. This figure far surpasses the results on abstinence reported for men from a variety of alcoholism treatment centers at their 18-month follow-up: If "long-term abstention were used as a criterion of remission, . . . only about one-fourth of these clients could be considered in remission by that definition" Armor, Polich, and Stambul (1976).[4]

Quantity of alcohol consumed

Overall, there is a shifting downward between the initial and follow-up interviews in the quantity the women usually drink. Initially, the women report usually consuming 10 drinks;[5] at follow-up this decreases to 6 drinks, ($p < .05$). This difference does not persist when the abstainers, or the abstainers combined with the rare-occasion drinkers, are removed from the total study group and only the quantity consumed by the current drinkers is considered. In fact, there is a slight increase to an average of 11 drinks, but this is not a significant difference. No difference then is found, on the average, in the amount consumed between the initial and follow-up interview for those women who continue to drink. The relationship between the abstainers alone and the abstainers combined with rare-occasion drinkers was examined by the various descriptive background variables, including the entry treatment settings.

Background variables and drinking outcome

In Table 7–1 are shown only those background variables for which there are significant differences by the drinking outcome. In this same table the two dimensions of drinking outcome, abstainers and abstainers combined with rare-occasion drinkers, are shown. In relation to the background variables, a significantly higher percentage of the professional women, of those in the highest socioeconomic group, and of white women are likely to be totally abstinent. When the abstainers are combined with those who drink only on rare occasions, the outcome continues to show significant improvement for these same subgroups. Since half of the 14 rare-occasion drinkers are among low-income women, this accounts in good measure for the improvement between the abstainers and the combined abstainers and rare-occasion drinkers in the low socioeconomic groups. It is only with the addition

TABLE 7-1 *Abstainers and Abstainers Plus Rare-Occasion Drinkers by Significant Background Variables and Description of Treatment: Percentage Distribution*

BACKGROUND VARIABLES AND TREATMENT			% ABSTAINERS		% ABSTAINERS (PLUS RARE-OCCASION DRINKERS)	
Background variables	Total	41	P Value	53		P Value
Professional status						
Professional		63	.05	71		.05
Nonprofessional		31		45		
Socioeconomic status						
High		64		75		
Middle		44	.001	51		.01
Low		17		34		
Race						
White		50	.05	63		.001
Black		13		22		
Residence						
Suburban		42	NS	60		.001
Urban		39		47		
Entry treatment agency						
Inpatient		38		49		
Outpatient		24	.001	40		.01
Alcoholics Anonymous		74		83		

of the category of rare-occasion drinkers, however, that the suburban women also show a significantly better drinking outcome; by abstinence alone no difference is found by the women's place of residence. The outpatient treatment group has a higher proportion of rare-occasion drinkers. Thus, in combining this group with the abstainers, the overall differences among the three types of treatment diminishes, although overall there continues to be a significant difference.

The very low percentage of black women shown in both categories of drinking outcome obviously requires comment. Only 13 percent of the black women are abstainers; this increases to 22 percent when both abstainers and rare-occasion drinkers are combined. Yet, no significant difference is found by current treatment and race; black women are just as likely to still be in treatment as the white women. A case-by-case review was done in an effort to better understand these results. Clearly, the black women have considerably fewer supports for a change in drinking; many continue to live in a setting where heavy drinking is the custom and to lack a supportive network of friends and family. It will be recalled that two-thirds of the black women are from the lower socioeconomic group, whereas the white women are from socioeconomic categories in almost equal proportions. Most of the black women, too, are currently living in very deprived life situations; some also are living with men who drink heavily and discourage any change in the study women's drinking.

Emotional health and drinking outcome

The interwoven relationship between emotional health and drinking behavior is well recognized and was discussed earlier in the chapter on the consequences of drinking. Heavy drinking will usually have an impact on emotional health although the converse is, of course, not true. Poor emotional health may lead to any number of other problems for women, not necessarily alcoholism. It was postulated that a reduction in drinking would bring about an improvement in the women's emotional health at the time of the follow-up, and it was noted in an earlier chapter that this did occur.

Table 7–2 presents the changes in emotional health scores between the initial and follow-up interviews. On the average, the women had 9.7 symptoms when entering treatment whereas at the time of the follow-up the average decreased to 5.8 symptoms. As discussed earlier, a score of seven or more denotes psychiatric impairment with some certainty (Langner, 1962). Thus the presence or absence of a significant difference between the two scores at the initial and the follow-up interviews should not be given so much weight in the interpretation as the presence of seven or more symptoms.

Those women whose drinking lessened at follow-up all show a dramatic and meaningful decrease in symptomatology, that is, fewer than seven symptoms. The original low-heavy–moderate-heavy and heavy–very heavy drinkers who are now abstainers have at present emotional health scale scores of 3.7 and 4.3, respectively. Even the heavy–very heavy subgroup who moved to the low-heavy–moderate-heavy drinking category report an average of 5.3 symptoms. Those three groups

TABLE 7–2 *Emotional Health Score and Quantity Drinking^a at Initial and Follow-up Interviews*

	FOLLOW-UP DRINKING (EMOTIONAL HEALTH MEAN: 5.8)		INITIAL DRINKING (EMOTIONAL HEALTH MEAN: 9.7)		
	Low-heavy–moderate-heavy (N=69)	Score		*Heavy–very heavy* (N=47)	Score
None (abstainers)	29	8.0(I) 3.7(F) *		18	10.6(I) 4.3(F) *
Low-heavy–moderate-heavy	27	9.4(I) 7.2(F) *		12	9.7(I) 5.3(F) *
Heavy–very heavy	13	9.5(I) 8.2(F) NS		17	12.4(I) 7.7(F) *

^{a} Very heavy, 15 or more drinks; heavy, 12–14; moderate-heavy, 5–11; low-heavy, less than 5; none, no drinking since the initial interview.
KEY: I = Initial interview
     F = Follow-up interview
* $p<.05$

who report drinking the same quantity approximately, or whose drinking increased at the time of the follow-up, continue to obtain a scale score of seven or more symptoms.

With one exception, the women's lower emotional health scores reflect a statistically significant improvement. The exception is that group of women who reported at the follow-up interview that they drink more than they did initially. These are the low-heavy to moderate-heavy drinkers whose drinking increased to either heavy or very heavy drinking at the follow-up. Initially reporting an average of 9.5 symptoms, they show relatively little improvement in symptomatology with a scale score of 8.2 at the follow-up. In contrast, the emotional health score of those women who stopped drinking, independent of the quantity they previously drank, is now within the normal range and can best be considered to reflect the end of the continuum showing only the mildest of symptomatology as measured by this scale.

These data raise several questions. The fact that most of the scores are significantly lower may be the result of regression effects towards the mean.[6] It may well be, too, that experiencing some form of treatment, or even acknowledging the need for treatment of their drinking problem, is in itself beneficial. Also, the results of treatment may be operating, along with spontaneous remissions. Some readers may consider the possibility that improved emotional health is the precursor of an alteration of drinking. Yet this consideration is not strongly persuasive since the change in symptomatology has occurred within a relatively brief period of time and involves women in varied treatment programs. What is most apparent is that it is only those women who are now abstaining and those who shifted from the heavy–very heavy category of drinkers to the low-heavy–moderate-heavy category who do not score at the level considered to reflect psychiatric impairment.

To attempt to explain this result, a regression analysis was carried out, and in Table 7–3 the results of this analysis are shown.[7] Five of the 29 variables entered in the analysis were found to have significant results and to explain an appreciable amount of the resulting change in the emotional health score at the follow-up, (R^2 adjusted, .493). Race, socioeconomic status, the emotional health score at the initial interview, entry into the study group from Alcoholics Anonymous, and the drinking outcome of abstainers and rare-occasion drinkers are found to be significant. Clearly, it is the emotional health score at the initial interview which made the most substantial contribution to the change reported in the emotional health score at the follow-up. Thus, the lower the emotional health scores at the initial interview, the greater the likelihood of a lower score at the follow-up. Entering the study from AA, being an abstainer or rare-occasion drinker and being

TABLE 7–3 *Regression Analysis of Emotional Health Scores at Follow-up*

	r	BETA
Race	−.39	−.16
Socioeconomic	−.42	.16
Emotional health at initial interview (Time 1)	.55	.42
AA entry treatment	−.36	−.18
Abstainers and rare drinkers	−.44	−.29

R	.718
R^2	.515
R^2 adjusted	.493
F ratio	23.345
d.f.	5; 110

white also contributed to the lower scores. Those in the lower socioeconomic group did have a higher emotional health score as well as having less change in their emotional health score between the initial and follow-up interviews.

Of considerable interest also is how the women themselves feel, independent of any measure we used to assess their emotional health. The results of the women's self-report is consistent with their emotional health score in that a majority of the women reported feeling better, 66 percent (scale score of 5) with an additional 21 percent feeling somewhat better (scale score of 6.5). In contrast, those few women, only four, who view themselves as much worse had an average score of 15 on the emotional health scale.

Employment and drinking outcome

Employment is quite important for many of the women since more than half depend on their own ability to earn a living for self-support. At the time of the follow-up interview, 50 of the women were the main wage earners of their households.

Employment is always considered an important indicator of behavioral change following treatment for drinking, and it seems no less important for this group of women since so few (27 percent) described themselves at the first interview as out of the labor force, either because they are students, housewives, or retired persons.

Although the overall percentage of study women employed does not differ appreciably between the initial and follow-up interviews, there was a great deal of shifting among the three categories of employed, unemployed, and those out of the labor force. When the data for only those women who were in the labor force at both time periods is examined, 44 percent are currently employed as compared with 38 percent at the time of the initial research interview. (This is not a statistically significant change based on the McNemar test of significance.) What differs primarily is that fewer considered themselves unemployed at the follow-up interview, probably because more do not see themselves as part of the labor force. Only a few of the background variables account for the shift. Professional women are significantly more likely to be employed, 71 percent as compared with 32 percent of the nonprofessional women ($p < .001$). The majority of women who were in AA as they entered the study are more likely to be employed at the follow-up, some 65 percent (p < .05). The professional women and those who sought help from AA are more likely to be employed; these findings are consistent with those of the initial interview.

The drinking outcome does not show any difference by the women's employment status. Thus, employed women are not significantly more likely to be abstainers than the other women, nor are they significantly more likely to be found among the combined abstainers and rare-occasion drinkers. Thus many of the currently employed women continue to be drinkers. In contrast to the unemployed women, more of the employed women are likely to be low-heavy or moderate-heavy drinkers (61 percent); the unemployed women are more likely to be heavy or very heavy drinkers (also 61 percent). Yet such a difference is not significant (p < .21). The currently employed women have fewer symptoms, and their emotional health scores can be considered in the normal range (average of 4.5 symptoms) while those of the unemployed are more likely to indicate psychiatric impairment (average of 7.4).

A further comment seems in order about the 27 women who are currently unemployed: Fourteen were unemployed at the initial interview and may be viewed by some as chronically unemployed. Yet the majority of the unemployed (some 70 percent) are still in treatment, and thus the outlook may be hopeful for an eventual return to work.

Prior treatment and drinking outcome

A majority of the study women, almost two-thirds, were treated for problem drinking prior to the first study research interview. Almost half of the women who had prior treatment were inpatients (46 percent), and many had also attended Alcoholics Anonymous (36 percent); a smaller percentage were seen as outpatients (18 percent). The duration of lifetime treatment was five weeks typically, if hospitalized; outpatient visits numbered 61 visits on the average or probably somewhat more than one year. Thus, an appreciable number of women have been treated for their problem drinking and some obviously for considerable periods of time. This, of course, does not represent continuous treatment.

As they entered treatment at the time of the research study, the emotional health scores of those given prior treatment reflected no differences when compared with those not given prior treatment. An exceedingly high proportion of abstainers (81 percent) were found to have had prior treatment, whereas one out of two (52 percent) of the non-abstainers had prior treatment. One clear implication of these findings for both the women and the treatment staff may be to view with some optimism the likely better outcome of a second, third, or even fourth treatment experience, even though prior treatment may not have had long-term beneficial results for the woman's drinking behavior.

Maintenance dosage of alcohol

Instead of designating reduced drinking for alcoholics as "normal" drinking, such a change might possibly be considered maintenance drinking. If one views an alcoholic as having developed a persistent need for the drug alcohol, then continuous but reduced drinking could be equated with a self-prescribed maintenance dosage. This seems to be a conceptually clearer and more valid characterization of what might be occurring for some individuals. The concept of maintenance obviously has been primarily applied to other drug abusers, particularly with the substitution of a controlled synthetic drug for the original one, for example, methadone as a replacement for heroin.

Such a concept may be useful if examined and applied in alcohol research. Substituting the concept of maintenance for "normal" drinking will call attention to the implications involved in patterned regular drinking. An implication embedded in this concept is that such drinking may exceed maintenance, an occurrence which cannot be predicted.

To determine if there is any evidence for the existence of a maintenance dosage of alcohol among the women seen at the follow-up interview, a review was carried out in the cases of those women who were classified as currently and usually drinking less than five drinks. Fifteen women were found in this category. Only 3 of the 15 drank this amount when seen initially. Most (nine) were formerly moderately heavy drinkers (5 to 11 drinks), and three were formerly heavy drinkers (12 to 14 drinks). Six of these 15 women are now classified as being rare-occasion drinkers and do not fit the concept of maintenance dosage, since the occasions for drinking are so few. Thus, only nine women are in fact eligible for consideration of their drinking as maintenance, and these nine are those discussed. Only one of the nine also drank less than five drinks when seen initially. The others were then classified as moderately heavy or heavy drinkers. The low-heavy drinker thus continues her low-heavy drinking, but she states this is now less frequent, one time every other week. The other eight report reducing the quantity they consume, and five of these eight do drink daily at the low-heavy level. The patterns for the others reflect great variability ranging from one to three times weekly to binge drinking.

It can be argued that the level reached by any reduction in drinking constitutes maintenance drinking and that the same logic applied to reviewing the lowest category of drinking used in the present study can also be applied to the other categories whenever drinking is reduced. Unfortunately, it is not possible to carry this discussion beyond the data available from the study women's self-reports. Blood alcohol levels and body weight should obviously be considered for a more rigorous examination of this issue. Gaining information in these areas, however, would need to be pursued with another study group.

Drinking outcome, emotional health score, and treatment

The same variables entered in the regression analysis to explain the emotional health score at the follow-up were also used to examine the drinking outcome.

Most of the women attended Alcoholics Anonymous at some point after becoming part of the study group. This aspect of treatment needed to be considered at each stage of the analysis. How did AA as a self-help group interact with the other treatment received, and what difference did it make in the outcome measures examined here: drinking behavior, emotional health, and employment?

A series of tables will illustrate the final pieces of the puzzle. First in Table 7-4 is shown the emotional health score at entry into treatment and follow-up by the type of treatment at entry: AA, inpatient plus AA, outpatient plus AA, inpatient alone, and outpatient alone. Most of the entry AA women also had additional treatment, but since there is no significant difference between the two groups in their emotional health scores, they are presented together.

The largest net change in emotional health score is that of the entry AA women, even though they were as impaired in their emotional health as those women who at entry into the study were inpatients and had had AA treatment. The next largest net change is achieved by those women who were outpatients and had had AA treatment, though they continue to have a score of more than 7 (7.35) at fol-

TABLE 7-4 *Emotional Health Score at Entry and Follow-up by Combinations of Treatment*

TYPE OF TREATMENT	NUMBER	ENTRY SCORE	FOLLOW-UP SCORE	NET CHANGE
Alcoholics Anonymous[a]	23	8.65	2.70	5.95
Inpatient plus AA	44	8.52	5.23	3.29
Outpatient plus AA	23	11.52	7.35	4.17
Inpatient alone	11	11.27	7.91	3.36
Outpatient alone	15	10.93	8.67	2.26
Total	N=116	9.72	5.85	3.87

F Test   2.377   7.587
$p=$ $<.057$ $<.001$

[a] All but nine of the entry AA women had additional treatment after entering the study group. Because there was no significant difference in their emotional health scores at follow-up, they are shown together in this table.

low-up. The F test shows a significant difference ($p < .001$) at the follow-up.

In Table 7-5 the effect by AA becomes clearer; for example, AA treatment combined with either inpatient or outpatient treatment shows 39 percent now abstaining as compared with the 15 percent who did not have AA treatment. The highest proportion of abstainers, as noted earlier, are those who entered from AA: 74 percent.

Abstinence was subsequently treated as an intervening variable between type of treatment and the emotional health score to explain the emotional health score. In Table 7-6 all those not abstaining have higher emotional health scores at follow-up than the abstainers. The highest emotional health score initially was that of the current non-abstainers who received no AA treatment (12.0). Compare this score

TABLE 7-5 *Alcoholics Anonymous and Abstinence: Percentage Distribution*

DRINKING OUTCOME	TOTAL	AA	ENTRY PLUS AA	ENTRY NO AA
	(N=116)	(N=23)	(N=67)	(N=26)
Abstainers	41	74	39	15
Non-Abstainers	59	26	61	85

$\chi^2 = 17.52$, 2df, $p<.001$

TABLE 7-6 *Emotional Health Scores, Alcoholics Anonymous, and Abstinence*

EMOTIONAL HEALTH	ENTRY AA	ENTRY PLUS AA	ENTRY NO AA
		Abstainers	
Initial	9.5	9.1	6.3
Follow-up	2.5	4.7	5.0
Change	−7.0	−4.4	−1.3
NS			
		Non-Abstainers	
Initial	6.2	9.9	12.0
Follow-up	3.3	6.8	9.0
Change	−2.9	−3.1	−3.0
NS			

with the other non-AA but now abstaining group whose emotional health score at both entry (6.3) and follow-up (5.0) is quite low—less than the score of 7, which reflects psychiatric impairment. This latter group of abstainers can be characterized as one of the "healthiest" emotionally as they entered treatment, as measured by this scale, and their emotional health score changed little, even with abstention. The non-abstainers have consistently higher emotional health scores at follow-up than the abstainers despite their entry scores; the change scores thus are not significant and there is a leveling in the AA groups.

Several questions are raised by this outcome. The emotional health scores of the first two abstaining groups are quite similar as they entered treatment with both having at least nine symptoms. Why is it that the abstaining entry AA women do so well? (They have a change of −7.0.) Yet, the entry AA group had as many symptoms (9.5) as those women who entered from inpatient or outpatient treatment and also had AA help (9.1). If we look to the AA experience alone to explain this result, it may be quite misleading since there were relatively few women who only had AA treatment (8 percent of the 116 women seen at the follow-up). An additional analysis in the next section on drinking outcome seems to clarify the contribution of AA and other treatment to the results reported.

Those women from the entry AA group who were not abstaining and whose emotional health score is so low should probably be discounted because of small numbers (N = 6). Both other groups of non-abstainers continue to have higher emotional health scores.

Drinking outcomes

Based on the regression analysis only the significant variables are shown in Table 7-7 and Table 7-8 as they relate to the abstainers and combined rare-occasion drinkers and abstainers. While a large part of the variance of 28.6 (R^2 adjusted) is accounted for by Alcoholics Anonymous at entry, and current attendance at Alcoholics Anonymous, several other variables persisted and contributed almost equally to the outcome; socioeconomic status, prior outpatient treatment and prior inpatient treatment.

Two variables negatively related to abstinence were additional outpatient and inpatient treatment; thus, these two subgroups were less likely to be abstainers.

In Table 7-8 showing the regression analysis for abstainers and rare-occasion drinkers, the variance explained increases to 38.2. Only four of the variables were found to be significant; race, additional outpatient or inpatient treatment (which were negatively correlated), and

TABLE 7-7 *Abstainers: Regression Analysis of Drinking Outcome*

SIGNIFICANT VARIABLES	r	BETA
Socioeconomic	.39	.18
Prior outpatient	.28	.17
Prior inpatient	.07	.20
Alcoholics Anonymous (entry)	.34	.19
Additional treatment		
Outpatient	−.24	−.21
Inpatient	−.25	−.19
Current treatment		
Alcoholics Anonymous	.37	.19

R	.569
R^2	.323
R^2 adjusted	.286
F ratio	8.680
d.f.	6; 109

TABLE 7-8 *Abstainers and Rare-Occasion Drinkers: Regression Analysis of Drinking Outcome*

SIGNIFICANT VARIABLES	r	BETA
Race	.31	.17
Additional treatment		
Outpatient	.28	−.17
Inpatient	.31	−.28
Current treatment		
Alcoholics Anonymous	.47	.43

R	.639
R^2	.409
R^2 adjusted	.382
F ratio	15.195
d.f.	5; 110

current treatment at Alcoholics Anonymous (which largely accounts for this outcome).

Finally, as seen in Table 7-9, those who had AA treatment only contributed little (.02) to the overall correlation explaining abstinence. Socioeconomic status and entry AA maintain their strong contribution while any outpatient treatment persists in its negative correlation.

TABLE 7-9 *Abstainers: Dependent Variable*

INDEPENDENT VARIABLES	r	BETA
Socioeconomic	0.39	0.30
Entry AA	0.34	0.42
Only AA treatment	0.02	−0.40
Any outpatient	−0.21	−0.26

multiple R	.551
multiple R^2	.303
F-ratio	12.08
d.f.	4; 111
p	.001

Conclusions

Some comment needs to be made here about some of the background variables and how they are related to the final results. In the single variable analysis, several relationships were shown originally (Table 7-1) as having statistically significant results when related to abstinence. Professional status, socioeconomic status, race, urban-suburban residence, and type of entry treatment. Except for socioeconomic status and entry from AA, these significant relationships did not persist when a large number of variables were entered into the regression analysis. While at various times these variables along with others such as marital status and age have been demonstrated to show differences in relation to some of the outcome measures used, they do not appear to be related to abstinence and the emotional health score. This may be as surprising as the fact that the quantity consumed does not relate to the outcome measures. Thus, such variables may loom as critical in determining who drinks and how much is consumed (Cahalan, Cisin, and Crossley, 1969), but they ultimately seem of minimal importance in who stops drinking.

Much of the data presented here concerning treatment outcome uses the most rigorous criteria, abstinence. After a period of approximately a year, we find a substantial proportion of the women meeting this criteria. Their numbers increase substantially, to more than half, when we combine the abstainers with those who drank only on rare occasions. Using the less rigorous outcome criteria of the time they had their last drink, a very high percentage are found not to be drinking in the month preceding the follow-up research interview (71 percent). In addition, there may be a number of women who can be considered to be "maintaining" themselves on a considerably decreased amount of alcohol. The concept of maintenance drinking is believed to be more valid than characterizing such drinkers as controlled or normal drinkers since inherent in the notion of maintenance drinking is the possibility that such drinking may exceed at some future date what is needed for avoiding discomfort.

There are some disturbing findings. Low-income women, and black women are considerably less likely to alter their drinking. These two groups are often the same. While this may not come as a surprise to those familiar with studies of treatment outcome, it serves to reinforce

Outcome of Treatment 153

the continuing jeopardy of the poor and minority women who, once becoming problem drinkers, are least likely to experience relief, even with treatment. Many of these women continue in treatment, without changing their drinking behavior appreciably. It was thought that this might mean that the settings have different goals. But almost without exception, the treatment settings state their goal for the patients to be abstinence, even though many do not provide the supports for such an outcome and do not believe the patient's chance for reaching such a goal to be very good. Because of the obstacles to improvement described earlier, both a different treatment approach and a more extensive duration of treatment may be needed for both low-income and/or minority women to overcome such extensive barriers to change which are rooted in their present life as much as in the past.

Given the range of treatment, the variety of settings incorporated in the study group, and the variability in the background of the women, such drinking outcomes may approximate well what can be expected, on the average, when women enter treatment for their drinking. The dramatic improvement in the women's emotional health score over time, most especially with a reduction in their drinking, bodes well for the futures of these women and for their capacities to cope with the variety of their future life tasks. Abstention is the overriding variable in explaining the women's improved emotional health rather than any of the background variables.

Notes

1. Based on returns for 124 women. Missing are three outpatient agency questionnaires. No questionnaires, of course, are available for the 23 women who entered the study from Alcoholics Anonymous. The selection of these treatment settings was described in Chapter 2.
2. The question to elicit binge drinking was: "Do you drink every day or go on binges and drink little in between?" The question allowed for the interviewer to explore other patterns of drinking, such as less than daily.
3. The definition of "rare occasion" involved primarily the frequency of drinking rather than the quantity consumed and consisted primarily of one occasion (for 8 of the 14 cases) but reached as much as an uninterrupted week of drinking, which then ceased. The time period of this drinking most typically followed discharge from a treatment program, or occurred on special occasions such as "toasting."
4. Armor, Polich, and Stambul's definition of remission includes classifying patients into the time periods at which abstinence began; using both the

previous month as well as a 6-month period of abstinence, and then adding the category of normal drinking, defined as typically 5 ounces or less or a daily intake of less than 3 ounces of ethanol, plus other changes in behavior. Based on these three groups (prior month, 6 months, normal), remission for 67 percent of the men was reported (p. 104).
5. In Chapter 5, 11 drinks were reported as the usual amount consumed. The difference between the 11 and 10 drinks reported in this chapter is due to the sample loss at follow-up.
6. Campbell and Stanley (1963, p. 181) observe this is likely to be a byproduct of an imperfect test–retest correlation when the subjects are selected because of their extreme scores. This observation may well partially explain the lower scores for all the women at the follow-up.
7. A number of variables were entered into a regression analysis to begin to explain the results reported here. Most of the same demographic variables used throughout the study were entered (never married, married now, age, suburban-urban residence, religion, professional or nonprofessional employment, socioeconomic status, and race). In addition to these variables, the specific type of prior treatment (inpatient, outpatient, and Alcoholics Anonymous), a similar classification for the entry treatment agencies, and any subsequent treatment using these same three categories. The emotional health scores at the initial interview and follow-up interview were also entered. The amount of drinking prior to the initial and follow-up interviews, binge drinking prior to the initial and follow-up interviews, employment status at the time of the initial and follow-up interviews, total abstinence, rare-occasion abstinence, and duration of drinking were also entered. These background and intervening variables were then related to the drinking outcome variables of abstinence and the rare-occasion users combined with abstainers, the emotional health score, and employment at the follow-up.

8
Conclusions and Summary: Implications for Intervention, Treatment, and Research

This research study is the first effort to study women as they entered a variety of settings for treatment of their alcoholism. The women of the study, who were seen in an initial interview in 1974, were seen again, on the average, one year later in a follow-up interview; by the middle of 1976, the basic data for the study were all collected. Consecutive admissions to 14 treatment agencies and several Alcoholics Anonymous groups were used to approximate a representative sample of alcoholic women entering treatment. Interviews with husbands, the study women's non-alcoholic sisters, and agency personnel who completed questionnaires at the two time periods also constituted the study's extensive data collection plan. Initially, 150 women were interviewed as they entered treatment; 116 of these same women were seen at the one year follow-up.

A review of the published research relating to alcoholic women in the early 1970s (see Chapter 1) led to the conclusion that no solid, descriptive data had been gathered on the treatment of alcoholic women—a first research priority for any study of women and their problems with alcohol. This resulted in the design of a study to examine:

1. The onset and etiology of problem drinking for women
2. The effects on self and family
3. Description of the course of treatment and outcome

Prior studies were typically based on small homogeneous samples. It was clear that a heterogeneous population of women should be studied although this could lead to other limitations if the subgroups studied became too small. To guard against such a possibility for at least two subgroups in whom there was interest, professional women were oversampled; also, the study group was initially stratified to represent both urban and suburban women. This sampling strategy assured sufficient numbers in at least these two subgroups. It was possible to analyze the data by a number of other subgroups for which data were previously lacking. In addition to the urban-suburban and professional women the data were also analyzed by the women's marital and employment status, socioeconomic status, race, age, marital status, religion, type of treatment at entry into the study, and the usual quantity of alcohol consumed. All of the critical descriptive areas discussed in earlier chapters were analyzed by these subgroups. Details of the categories within each of these variables are discussed in Chapter 2 in the analysis plan.

The lack of substantial studies on women is rivaled in a number of other areas besides alcoholism. Yet, since the most basic data about alcoholic women did not exist at the time this study was designed, the examination of the descriptive data was seen as the first critical step in understanding alcoholic women in treatment and would need to precede testing of hypotheses about alcoholic women. The need for control groups or norms was also recognized as critical, and in the present study a number of comparisons are made with a smaller group of non-alcoholic sisters of the women interviewed.

This final chapter is organized around the study's original objectives and will focus not only on the averages found in a number of areas but on the differences established among the subgroups. Although some of the findings fit our expectations, our analysis by the various subgroups enables somewhat more precision in presenting descriptive data on alcoholic women than has been possible heretofore.

The findings from this study should be viewed only as a starting point in our current understanding of alcoholic women in treatment.

Replication will be needed in a number of areas. Some of the problems of measurement encountered need resolution and refinement. The conceptualization of alcoholism in women seems especially in need of reexamination. Cross-dependence with other drugs for women is only beginning to be studied, and it is often not clear which dependence comes first. Is alcoholism a variation of the same underlying phenomenon, but with a different substance? Other drugs may be taken to intensify the effects of alcohol. Such knowledge is needed to ensure a satisfactory withdrawal, but a multiple dependency may have the same treatment course as a single dependency.

The onset and etiology of problem drinking for women
ONSET OF DRINKING

Most of the women were drinking by the time they were 21. Many, however, began their drinking at a much younger age, but some began as late as their fifth decade. On the whole, the women were usually in their late 30s by the time they entered treatment, although the average age at which their drinking problems began was 33 years. There seems to be support in this study for a relatively short interval between recognition of a drinking problem and the attempt to get help. Although the average was 6 years, more than half the women (56 percent) presented themselves for treatment in fewer than 5 years after becoming aware that a drinking problem had developed. Thus, some alcoholic women may be less reluctant to obtain treatment than previously thought.

But then the question arises: "Why are they not seen in treatment settings in the numbers reported to exist in the population?" There is no evidence in this study to support a rapid progression of alcoholism in women. These aspects of alcoholism in women, namely, the interval between social and problem drinking and the progression of alcoholism, have often been considered telescoped when compared with those of men. Comparisons with men can be made only when women and men from the same treatment settings are compared and in the same time frame or where there is a sufficient accumulation of studies from differing time periods and geographic locations to support the existence of differing time intervals for women and men on the progression to problem drinking and alcoholism.

The existence of a stressful event has often been cited as associated with alcoholism in women; this has not been given any particular emphasis in studies of men. Almost half of the study women could not offer any specific life situation that precipitated their drinking problem. Based on the present study, then, there is insufficient evidence to document a specific life situation as being associated with alcoholism in women. The husband interviews support this interpretation. Yet the evidence is sufficiently persuasive of the existence of a specific stress for a large number of women to warrant study of this aspect of alcoholism in the future. At the same time, it might be more meaningful to offer a comparison with men alcoholics to see if stress is truly gender related. It may well be associated with subgroups of women and men problem drinkers and their shifting to heavier drinking may quite possibly be associated with early symptoms of depression for both women and men.

Because alcoholic women are so heavily censured by society for their condition, it is understandable that a specific life situation is so often cited in the literature when they are discussed, since such a view shifts responsibility to an outside event. Given our present state of knowledge, however, it seems preferable to understand the course of alcoholism as an ill-defined illness rather than to look for causation in a given life situation. Indeed, there may in reality be two or more "illnesses" present for *some* alcoholic women: depression and alcoholism. Both may require separate but coordinated treatment.

Alcoholic drinking is usually thought to involve heavy drinking as defined by whoever wishes to define heavy. Earlier in this study, it was shown that not all alcoholic women consume the "heavy" quantities associated with alcoholism. Also, the "set and setting" of drinking may be quite important for women, even more important than for men, because of society's emotional and moral taboos placed on drinking by women. The concept of heavy drinking would seem to be quite loose, ill-defined, and possibly lacking in utility. Certain aspects of the effects of alcohol are quite unique to the individual. This statement is not meant to be confused with the physiological effects of slurred speech, balance, and so on, on which most observers could agree. For example, a female member of a religious order may report usually drinking three drinks several times weekly and feel the need to seek treatment for alcoholism. The taboos against drinking for such a religious person are far greater than those experienced by other women.

Conclusions and Summary 159

The response then to alcohol and tolerance for alcohol may be considerably different when compared with that of other women. Even the measurement of blood alcohol levels is not achieved strictly by a weight-consumption ratio in either women or men; it can be influenced by individual tolerance. It has been suggested, in fact, that the "heavy" alcohol consumer can drink more than a "moderate" user and still have the same blood level of alcohol (Ray, 1978).

As described in Chapter 3, 83 percent of the women usually drank five or more drinks at the time they entered treatment (see Table 3–2). Those who usually drink less than five drinks represent a considerable proportion of women who came for treatment for a drinking problem (17 percent). As argued earlier, the definition of heavy drinking applied in national surveys (five or more), is not an adequate concept when applied to women.

There has been much interest in the frequency of drinking, and this often is a major consideration when individuals examine their drinking to assess if drinking involves a dependency pattern. Most recent classfication schemes of drinking take account of the frequency of the occurrence (Cahalan, Cisin, and Crossley, 1969). Yet there clearly seems to be a group of individuals whose drinking is less than daily such as weekend drinkers, or even those with longer intervals in between, who are referred to most commonly as binge drinkers. Alcoholic women cannot be easily dichotomized into either daily or binge drinkers. Thus frequency of drinking does not seem to be a critical variable in the analysis of the data but rather it is shown repeatedly that the usual quantity consumed is most important and this has its most meaningful implications in the consequences of drinking.

The stereotypes of women are many, but the "housewife" mythology is more extensive, it seems, than others. Although interest remains high in the alcoholic housewife, research studies specific to the housewife do not exist. Based on our present research data, we claim that in most ways she does not differ from the other alcoholic women in any way but one: she is more likely to drink alone than the working women who are not married. And both of these subgroups of women are more likely to report drinking alone when compared with the *unemployed* women who are not married.

More refined interpretations must await future empirical studies. Here we suggest that these women—housewives and working women who are not married—may be more likely to hide their drinking from others because they have meaningful ties in marriage or work relationships they wish to safeguard.[1] Obviously this interpretation could also apply to other women with meaningful relationships such as women in religious orders, single women living with their children, women who live with adult relatives such as parents, lesbians, or women living with men but not married.

This interpretation seems to find support in the analysis of the women's socioeconomic status; for, the higher the socioeconomic status of the woman, the more likely she is to drink alone. Such women and their families usually have a major investment in adhering to social norms that tend to be more rigid. What emerges, then, is a pattern of many women doing much of their drinking alone, and drinking less than they usually do with others. The social situation in which drinking is done is of considerable interest. The women, too, only drink their usual quantity when with close friends. Many (61 percent) report having close friends with drinking problems and changing friends as their drinking alters.

As they entered treatment, the study women were most likely to have escapist rather than social reasons for their drinking, but there was one subgroup for which there was a notable exception. Black women still maintained significantly higher social reasons for their drinking as well as having escapist reasons. Thus, there may be a different reason for the persistence of drinking among black women, one that may also be a clue to some of the differential findings relating to treatment outcome. What may be needed to best understand these data is a study of the social meaning of alcohol to the black community and most particularly to black women. The key question is whether or not this meaning persists even for those with drinking problems. It has been suggested that the social context of drinking for blacks may have quite a different meaning because of their special history in the United States (Harper, 1976). If this social meaning of drinking is used to solidify and increase cohesiveness in the black community, then it might serve that purpose even more for black women who have traditionally been the most isolated.

The use of other drugs in combination with alcohol is found to be increasingly common among women. The synergistic effects that result when one drug, such as alcohol, is added to other drugs, such as tranquilizers and sedatives, to form more complex but unpredictable interactions, are still poorly understood. Little good epidemiological data exists on such female drug-taking behavior, and almost no major research studies exist in this area. Yet because of the high risk women have of overdoses of alcohol plus other drugs, it is an area that clearly requires high priority in research. There are some major differences found in the present group of study women when the subgroups were analyzed. Many took tranquilizers (42 percent) and sleeping pills (24 percent) while drinking, the two drugs most likely to have synergistic effects. Using a mean score of other drug usage, the highest other drug usage with alcohol was found among white women as compared to black, those who usually drink more than 15 drinks daily and women under 30. Obviously, these groups run a higher risk than others of experiencing overdoses from taking alcohol in combination with other drugs. What may be an additional surprise in these findings is the lack of variation by socioeconomic status. Women in all socioeconomic groups are equally likely to engage in drug taking with alcohol. And, we are talking mostly about legal drug use, the psychoactive drugs prescribed by physicians.

ETIOLOGY OF DRINKING FOR WOMEN

Little is yet known about what causes alcoholism. The case has been made throughout this study for applying current knowledge to the data such as the now widely accepted definition of alcoholism encompassing either psychological or physiological dependency, but not requiring the existence of both. It is known that alcoholism is more prevalent in some countries than in others. Yet, a review of ethnographic studies points to its existence primarily in Western cultures (Heath, 1975, p. 56).

As in other studies citing the family background of alcoholic women, a high percentage of women in the present study (61 percent) also indicate they have one or more relatives with a drinking problem, and almost two-fifths have one or more parents with a drinking problem. Obviously, parents or relatives may provide the necessary role model for alcoholic women. Yet relatively few of the women had sisters with a drinking problem. Thus, even in the presence of such role models, becoming alcoholic seems highly individualistic. Where does this fit with alcoholism as learned behavior or alcoholism as a disease? Since so many of the women, almost half, did not cite a specific life situation preceding problem drinking, this is not seen as a major unitary explanation of alcoholism in women. Yet 51 percent did cite life situations that could be construed as emotional losses, which may point to a group of alcoholic women who have responded with alcoholic drinking to such losses.

The interviews with 33 non-alcoholic sisters were most useful in relation to guarding against false conclusions; in addition, they supported—and in a sense validated—descriptions of family drinking and problem drinking. Most of the sisters constituted a normal group against which the alcoholic women could be assessed. The concept of "normal" is used here in the broadest sense in relation to the non-alcoholic sisters. The interviewed sisters did not have a drinking problem and were selected to be interviewed for this reason. Most of the matched non-alcoholic sisters do drink, but they do so in fairly light quantities, and their reasons for drinking are primarily social, rather than the escapist reasons given by the study women. An assessment made of their emotional health also indicates that the majority are free of symptoms usually considered to be indicators of psychiatric impairment; in contrast, almost all of their matched alcoholic sisters whose emotional health was assessed similarly on entry into treatment were found to have such psychiatric impairment.[2]

The present life situation of the sisters contrasted sharply with that of the study women as they entered treatment. The major measurable difference was in marital status; similar proportions of the matched sisters married at some point, but the majority of non-alcoholic sisters continued in their marriage and the alcoholic women did not. A further facet of their behavior is worth noting. The use of other drugs, especially tranquilizers, is significantly higher for the alcoholic women. Thus, in contrast with their sisters, this usage is quite dramatic and serves to reinforce the vulnerability of alcoholic women to the dangerous usage of potentially fatal drugs with alcohol.

Questions relating to possible role confusion reveal some tenuous support for the conclusion that the study women perceive their parents differently than do their non-alcoholic sisters. They recall receiving less approval from their parents.

The use of the sisters as controls is viewed as preventing the emergence of further speculation about the alcoholic women which would

Conclusions and Summary

ultimately be inaccurate. The value of this approach is also most evident in Anderson's study of the patterns of sex-role identification in the pair-matched sisters (1976). In using the more rigorous control group of the matched sisters in the present study, Anderson replicated the work of Wilsnack (1973). No support emerged for the contention that alcoholic women are more masculine than non-alcoholic women in unconscious identification. In fact, both the alcoholic women and their sisters were more masculine than the female norm.

There is agreement between the matched sister pairs on almost every area reviewed in their different life stages. The data strongly indicate a less satisfying current life situation for the study women. There is a suggestion, too, that early parental relationships were less satisfying for the alcoholic women. What seems to happen is that adult life experiences are also less satisfying, and this is especially evident in the outcome of their marriage. We did not attempt to assess this area of adult relationships except in a general way. This is believed to point the way to an area needing further research. When the study women married, they tended also to choose heavy-drinking men in contrast to their sisters who were more likely to marry light-drinking men. Each non-alcoholic sister comments repeatedly on her marriage as being quite different from that of her alcoholic sister's; generally she speaks positively about her own marriage. Thus marriage can be considered a benign or positive adult experience for the sisters as compared to that of the study women.

It can also be argued that in choosing the traditional route of marriage, the study women may have further reinforced conflict for themselves. In a sense, most of the study women have failed in their marital relationship, a failure that most of them see, it will be recalled, as independent of their drinking.

Effects on self and others
EFFECTS ON SELF

For most women, the negative consequences of their drinking are considerable at the point they entered treatment. Chapter 4 on the consequences of drinking documented the extensive job, health, family, and social ramifications, which they readily acknowledged. What emerged as a key variable relating to the consequences of drinking was the quantity consumed.

Hiding their drinking, leading a relatively isolated existence, or changing friends to allow their heavy drinking to be pursued without interruption was a fairly common theme. Most had experienced an alcoholic "blackout"—a loss of memory while drinking; some had also put themselves (and others) in great danger as they drove at high speeds. Twenty-one percent had road accidents because of drinking, and this was even higher for the suburban women. More common even were injuries while drinking, such as falls and burns. Since they experienced considerable criticism from others because of their drinking, they believe women to be more rejected than men for their heavy drinking. Their emotional status is poor, and the average number of symptoms, indicating psychiatric impairment, quite high. They seem to have little recognition of their increased tolerance for alcohol, which requires more alcohol to achieve the same effects, and its increasing negative impact.

Suicide attempts directly attributed to drinking are quite high for the study women (27 percent). Depression may seem to be the paramount illness as the study women enter treatment. A review of their symptoms in the classical psychiatric sense can easily lead to a diagnosis of depression because many are isolated from friends, have difficulty sleeping, have strong feelings of hopelessness, and show poor concentration. But such a mistaken diagnosis easily leads to an incorrect therapy program, one that may account for the continuing disillusionment of some with professional care; for, it seems clear that depressive symptoms in reality oftentimes mask alcoholism, which is the primary illness. It is only after alcohol is withdrawn for some time and the woman's life is stabilized again that a differential diagnosis is possible between depression and alcoholism. Yet a careful history should assist considerably in distinguishing the two diagnoses. In both instances, however, withdrawal from alcohol is needed.

The chapter on the results of treatment shows in detail the marked decrease in such symptomatology when there is a reduction in drinking. What is now needed are longitudinal studies to distinguish firmly between causes and effects. Yet the inference based on the present data is clear: Much of the symptomatology and harmful behavior of the alcoholic women is directly attributable to the consumption of alcohol and those women who consume more than 15 drinks usually experience the most severe consequences.

EFFECTS ON OTHERS

In contrast to the woman's own social, psychological, and physiological problems, alcoholism may also have a direct impact on those living or working with her. This is an aspect of the consequences of alcoholism that has often been difficult to measure. Those living with an alcoholic woman actually do not remove themselves. There is no evidence from this study that husbands of alcoholic women are any more likely to leave their wives than are the husbands of non-alcoholic wives. Those husbands interviewed seem to still maintain a loyalty, to express hope and love; or they seem committed to the relationship because of the presence of children. Many of the children themselves are thought to be affected by the study women. Yet the measures used to examine the effects on the social and school activities of the children do not elicit any differences between the children of the alcoholic women and those of their non-alcoholic sisters. Based on present knowledge, one can only infer here that such children are at high risk for developing alcoholism. Again, only as a result of longitudinal studies is adequate data possible in this area. Until then, information based on individual experiences, which may be misleading, will be the major data source.

Description of the course of treatment and outcome

Since the preceding chapter was devoted solely to the results of treatment, the interested reader might wish to return to that chapter for the detailed discussion of treatment and its results. What is apparent from this study is the rather remarkably good drinking outcome for so many of the women. The fact that as many as 71 percent had not been drinking in the month preceding the follow-up interview may well be a precursor of a considerably altered life. The appreciable numbers of the women who had some experience with AA, in addition to inpatient or outpatient treatment, may well be an indicator, too, of the usefulness for many of such a supportive group experience.

An appreciable decrease of psychiatric symptoms is concomitant with a reduction of drinking. There was no overall change in employment for the women, but this was found not to be a good indicator of altered functioning for women as a group. It may, however, prove to be in the near future as more women join the labor force. Most of the women who worked continued to do so despite their drinking and, in a number of instances, the employers' awareness of their drinking problems.

Conclusions

This has been a study of alcoholic women in treatment. In the tradition of research, it grew out of an earlier study (Corrigan, 1974a) in which women with drinking problems were identified as "different" from men. The major difference observed at that time was the heightened secrecy of the women. The present study, taking its direction from this earlier work, is descriptive and exploratory. What emerges is the extensive psychological and physiological manifestations of the women's dependence on alcohol. As they entered treatment there was almost no awareness on their part that such a dependency existed. Also, what is most evident is the need for women to begin to examine why they are so overly ready to accept mind-altering substances such as alcohol and other drugs.

Scientific knowledge has always been slow in reaching and gaining acceptance among the general population. Although recent surveys point to the American public's better understanding of the effects of alcohol, these same surveys underscore the lack of change in attitudes towards alcoholism. Much of the population (fully two-thirds) continue to view alcoholism as a moral problem (Johnson et al., 1977). Since women have always been perceived as upholding and perpetuating the moral standards of society, their nonconformity to these standards are, indeed, judged harshly. Thus women have been given unique responsibilities. The connection between the individual person—in this instance the alcoholic woman—and such high and possibly unrealistic expectations has always been ambiguous. But, the deviation for a woman from society's moral standards quite clearly seems to result in a differential perception of her behavior. Alcoholic women, like all women, have internalized this differential perception. Nowhere is this more evident than in the preceding pages. Change may occur when both women and men equally share in responsibility for societal standards and when the perception of alcoholism is moved out of the moral domain and into the mainstream of the dependencies.

Notes

1. If we define "housewife" to include only those women who are married and not employed outside the home, then, 81 percent of such women are likely to drink alone.
2. For those women whose drinking altered, this psychiatric impairment did not persist one year later.

APPENDIX A
Data Base

INTERVIEW SCHEDULES

Six schedules were prepared for the study: the initial interview with each of 150 study women, and a follow-up interview after one year; a sister and husband interview; finally, two agency schedules describing treatment for both the initial and follow-up phase.

Women subjects (first interviews and follow-up interviews). The data collected was extensive and this book essentially contains data from the first interview which focused on each woman's history and pattern of drinking, other drug use, consequences of drinking, family history of drinking, comparative data on non-alcoholic sisters, and identification of factors leading to treatment. The intent was to obtain good descriptive data in a number of critical areas as well as possible explanatory information about alcoholism in women. These interviews usually took two hours to complete.

The follow-up interview was used to gather the woman's history of treatment, which was not possible during the lengthy first interviews. Also a description of the course of treatment subsequent to the first interview was obtained; by using various scales it was possible to measure the women's feelings of well-being at the time of the initial and the follow-up interviews, especially their emotional health. The Franck drawing test (Anderson, 1976) and other measures were used to replicate a previous study (Wilsnack, 1973). Much of this follow-up interview is presented in summarized form in the chapter on treatment outcome.

Non-alcoholic sister interviews. The sister interviews contained similar life-experience questions asked of the study women about childhood, adolescence, and their adult years. Along with answers to these questions, a drinking and drug-use history was obtained. We also posed a series of questions to assist in understanding the development of heavy drinking by the women now in treatment. This interview extended, on the average, over one hour.

Husband interviews. As with the sisters, many of the key questions asked of the women were repeated in interviews with the husbands; for example, the effect of drinking on their marriage and children, on their sexual relationship, and the steps taken to secure help. These interviews were completed in less than an hour usually.

Agency questionnaires. Questionnaires were also used with the agencies at the beginning and termination of treatment. Each initial treatment questionnaire was completed by the responsible agency staff members within one month of a patient's first appointment or admission.

The questionnaire completed at the termination of treatment elicited data about the professional background of the staff providing treatment, type of treatment, duration of treatment, services provided, plan at termination, staff goals, and success in achieving these goals. The patient's motivation and family involvement in treatment were also measured. Finally, a systematic evaluation was made of each patient's family relations, job functioning, and health and social relations.

INTERVIEWERS

A total of 21 interviewers were involved in the interviewing of the women, sisters, and husbands. All but one were female, and most of

Appendix A

them had a master's degree in social work. All had considerable interviewing experience, and many in research interviewing. In addition, 12 interviewers from family or alcoholism treatment agencies in other states were involved in interviewing sisters and study women at the time of follow-up.

INTERVIEWING PROCEDURES

To facilitate the interviewing process and to enhance the relationships with agency staff, one, or at most two, interviewers were assigned to each agency. Interviewers were available at the agency site to conduct interviews at the time of the first admission interview on the outpatient service or, if the woman respondent could not remain for the more extended time needed for the research interview, she was offered the option of being seen at home or when she next returned to the agency. Outpatients were interviewed within the first month of agency registration even if they did not return for a second agency visit, either because they were referred elsewhere or chose not to keep a second appointment. Where possible, inpatients were interviewed prior to discharge, allowing sufficient time for detoxification. In most cases, they were seen from 4 days to 3 weeks after their admission.

RESPONSE TO RESEARCH: COMPARISON OF THE
INTERVIEWED AND NOT-INTERVIEWED SUBJECTS

All those who were asked to give their assistance (agency directors, staff, alcoholic women, sisters, and husbands) were approached with the explanation that research relating to alcoholism has been conducted to date primarily with men and thus our knowledge of alcoholism is derived from studying men alcoholics. To understand alcoholism in women it is necessary to interview women and those who know them. We need their help. Almost without exception, such an approach met with success; refusals were minimal. Where such refusals did occur, we assessed what differences might exist between the interviewed and those who were not interviewed.

Although we interviewed 150 women as planned, there were an additional 21 women at the agencies who were eligible for the study. Some of the women who refused to be interviewed did not acknowledge drinking as a problem or did not wish to discuss drinking. Other major reasons for not interviewing the women was that they were transferred to another facility before the interview could be completed, that they signed out against medical advice, or that they never returned to the agency after agreeing to be interviewed.

It was possible to obtain demographic data on 16 of these 21 women from the agencies and to compare them on the same data with the 150 study women. When age, education, race, religion, employment status, occupation, income, living situation, and previous treatment were compared, no significant differences were found between the two groups.

Table A–1 shows the potential subject pool of sisters and husbands and the women at the time of follow-up. In each instance, the subjects not interviewed were compared with those interviewed on the 10 variables described in the analysis plan in Chapter 2. No significant differences were found when the interviewed sisters were compared with those not interviewed on these variables.

There was only one significant difference in the background of the study husbands interviewed when contrasted to those not interviewed. We were more successful in interviewing suburban husbands and less successful with those from the urban study group. Thus 90 percent of

TABLE A–1 *Sisters, Husbands, and Women Seen At Follow-up: Numbers of Completed Interviews*

SUBJECT POOL	SISTERS	HUSBANDS	WOMEN AT FOLLOW-UP
No sister/husband	*52*	*103*	
Alcoholic sister only	*11*	—	
Women refused permission	*31*	*14*	
Total available subjects	*56*	*33*	*150*
Sister/husband refused[a]	14	6	—
Could not locate[b]	7	7	—
Interviewed	35[c]	20	116
Percent complete available subjects	(62.5)	(60.6)	(77)

[a] Includes two sisters too young to be interviewed.
[b] Includes one husband who died after the woman respondent gave permission and two who were separated from their wives at the time of the attempted interview.
[c] One sister identified herself as having an earlier drinking problem; a second sister interview was returned by an out-of-state agency as incomplete. Thus, only 33 usable interviews are cited in the study.

Appendix A

the interviewed husbands were from the suburban area, whereas they represented 72 percent of those originally available.

FOLLOW-UP INTERVIEWS

The study design called for the reinterviewing of women one year after the initial interview. Because of the extensive period of initial interviewing required, however, subjects were actually interviewed from 8 to 22 months after their first interview with an average of 13 months elapsing. Throughout the study, the women were informed that their participation was voluntary and that the interviews were based upon their agreement to be seen. At the point that the interviewer was assigned to a particular woman for a follow-up interview, a contact to arrange a convenient appointment was made by telephone, or in case of no telephone, a letter was sent asking the woman to contact the interviewer by placing a collect call to a specified telephone number. If there was no response to these attempts to make contact, the interviewer had the choice of making either an announced or unannounced visit to the address.

This approach resulted in 116 completed interviews. The 116 subjects located and interviewed at follow-up differed from the 34 subjects not interviewed on two of the 10 major variables used in the study: socioeconomic (SES) and agency status (Table A-2). The interviewed women were somewhat more likely to be found in the high SES group than in the low. The greatest loss among those not interviewed was found among women in the lowest SES, 53 percent, whereas they comprised less than two-fifths of the original study group. The original type of entry agency of the women explains this outcome at follow-up. None of the original AA members were lost to the follow-up. We then reanalyzed SES, omitting the AA members, and found no difference between the subjects initially interviewed and those seen at follow-up on SES. It appears then that the AA subjects, 14 of whom are in the highest SES, accounted for the significant difference in SES at follow-up. When agency status was also reanalyzed, omitting AA members, the significant difference by agency status also disappears. What this means is that our losses at follow-up were equally distributed between inpatients and outpatients, whereas the AA members are fully represented.

TABLE A-2 *Comparison of Characteristics of Study Women Interviewed and Not Interviewed at Follow-up: Percentage Distribution*

CHARACTERISTIC	TOTAL STUDY (N=150)	PERCENT NOT INTERVIEWED (N=34)	PERCENT INTERVIEWED (N=116)	P
Age (mean years)	41	38	41	NS
Locale				
Suburban	41	29	45	NS
Urban	59	71	55	
Professional employment				
Yes	27	15	30	NS
No	73	85	70	
Marital status				
Married	31	21	34	
Separated	11	15	10	
Divorced	20	26	18	NS
Widowed	11	12	10	
Never married	27	26	28	
Marital and employment status				
Married–employed	10	9	10	
Married–not employed	21	12	24	
Not married–employed	26	17	28	NS
Not married–not employed	43	62	38	
Socioeconomic status (SES)				
Low	39	53	35	
Middle	34	35	34	.05
High	27	12	31	
Socioeconomic status (omitting AA)	(N=127)		(N=93)	
Low	43	53	40	
Middle	36	35	36	NS
High	21	12	24	
Race	(N=144)	(N=33)	(N=111)	
White	78	73	79	NS
Black	22	27	21	
Religion				
Protestant	44	35	47	
Catholic	47	53	45	NS
Other	9	12	8	

Appendix A

TABLE A–2 (*Continued*)

CHARACTERISTIC	TOTAL STUDY (N=150)	PERCENT NOT INTERVIEWED (N=34)	PERCENT INTERVIEWED (N=116)	P
Agency status				
Inpatient	49	53	47	
Outpatient	36	47	33	.05
AA	15	—	20	
Agency status (omitting AA)	(N=127)		(N=93)	
Inpatient	58	53	59	NS
Outpatient	42	47	41	
Usual quantity of drinks				
Very heavy (15 or more drinks)	25	35	23	
Heavy (12–14 drinks)	18	18	18	NS
Moderately heavy (5–11 drinks)	40	32	42	
Low-heavy (less than 5 drinks)	17	15	17	

DATA CODING

After completed questionnaires were edited, the responses to open-ended questions were recorded to form the basis of coding categories. Precoded data, which encompassed about one-half of each interview, required only transfer to the code sheets. Coders were trained in small groups, and a total of five were utilized in the study. When coders were uncertain about a response, they were instructed to list the case, card, and column number of each problem on a problem sheet. These sheets were reviewed by the coding supervisor, discussed with the coder, and the problems resolved on each case before coding was resumed on a new case.

To insure reliability in the coding of the initial interview with the alcoholic women, 10 percent (N=15) of these cases were randomly selected and double-coded. Disagreements were resolved independently by a third coder, and errors were recorded by card and column number. Where errors were identified in any column critical to the analysis these were recorded as such in each code book in use. Consistency checks were done on all 150 cases, and errors were corrected after being reviewed by the coding supervisor. Identical procedures were used to establish reliability in the coding of the sister, husband, and homeless women interviews and of the follow-up interviews with the alcoholic women.

APPENDIX B
Statistical Procedures

Explanatory notes on the statistical procedures used are presented here in the order in which they appear in the chapters. The computer program used was primarily SPSS (Statistical Package for the Social Sciences, Nie, et al., 1975). Certain new programs were developed by the study's statistical consultants Jane Li and later John Grundy. The study programmer, Harriet Fink, guided the use of the many card sets and tapes needed for a given program. The explanations for these tests were selected primarily from the SPSS manual and from Siegel (1956).

Statistical significance: the probability that the observed relationship as reported in any study could have occurred by chance. In social science research, the tradition has developed to accept as statistically significant relationships that have a probability of occurring by chance 5 percent of the time or less, that is, five out of 100 samples, ($p < .05$ or $< .01$, or $< .001$); or, put another way, there is a chance of being wrong five times out of a 100. Tests of significance indicate only the likelihood that an observed relationship actually does exist. They usually do not tell us how strong the relationship is. Also, a relationship may be statistically significant without being substantively important, that is, a statistically significant relationship may exist between two variables and at the same time be deemed of little importance by a reader.

The mean: the sum of the scores divided by the total number of cases. It is most commonly referred to as the average.

Chi square: a test of statistical significance to determine whether a systematic relationship exists between two variables. If there is no relationship, then any deviation found is very likely due to chance. It allows us to infer if variables are related or independent. After computing expected cell frequencies, they are then compared to the actual frequency values found. The greater the difference between the expected and the observed frequencies the larger the chi square.

Except for age all variables shown in Table 2–4 are at the nominal level, meaning no value is attached to the categories, which are merely labeled ("race," "age," "locals," and so on). The statistical test for most of the relationships between variables is chi square. The test for age is a t test.

t test: a test to determine whether or not it is reasonable to conclude that a difference exists between the two samples means, and where such a difference exists, it implies a true difference in the parent population. The t test is for equality/inequality of the mean.

Sign test: the sign test is used to establish if the (two) conditions were different for the paired sisters. It uses plus and minus signs rather than quantitative data. Different pairs can be used as was done with the sisters; or each person can be her own control.

Standard deviation: a measure of the dispersion around the mean. It is the square root of the variance.

F value (or t value): a test of significance. The F value is a statistical test for the equality of group variances. (Variance is a statistic that measures how closely specific cases in a group or category cluster about the mean). It is similar to a t test, but it is applied when there are more than two categories involved. By using this one test, it is possible to determine if there are differences among the categories.

Student-Newman-Keuls range test: a systematic procedure for comparing all possible pairs of group means. This is a very important statistical test for a study such as the present one in which comparisons are made *after* the data are obtained.

McNemar test: a test for nominal scale measurement. The McNemar test is also used for two related samples, such as matched pairs.

Wilcoxin matched-pairs signed-ranks test: a test using information about the direction of the difference within pairs. The Wilcoxin test gives more weight to a pair that shows a large difference between the two conditions than to a pair that shows a small difference. It allows ranking the differences in order of absolute size.

Cramer's V: a measure of association. Cramer's V tells how strongly two variables are related to each other. It measures the extent to which characteristics of one sort and characteristics of another sort go together. It also indicates the extent to which prior knowledge of a case value on one variable enables a researcher to predict the case's value on the other variable.

Multiple regression: a procedure to study the linear relationship between a set of independent variables and a dependent variable while taking into account the interrelationship among the independent variables. The basic goal of multiple regression is to produce a linear and additive combination of independent variables which will correlate as highly as possible with a dependent variable. This linear combination can then be used to "predict" values of the dependent variable in question, and the importance of each of the independent variables in that prediction can be roughly assessed.

Bibliography

Acker, J. 1973. Women and social stratification: A case of intellectual sexism. In *Changing Women in a Changing Society*, J. Huber, ed. University of Chicago Press, Chicago.

Amark, C. A. 1951. A study in alcoholism—clinical, social-psychological and genetic investigations. *Acta Psychiatr. Neurol., 70* (suppl. 2): 1–283.

Anderson, S. C. 1976. Patterns of sex role identification in alcoholic women. Ph.D. Dissertation, Rutgers University.

Armor, D. J., Polich, J. M., and Stambul, H. B. 1976. *Alcoholism and Treatment*. Rand Corporation, Santa Monica, Calif.

Bailey, M. B. 1967. Psychophysiological impairment in wives of alcoholics as related to their husbands' drinking and sobriety. In *Alcoholism—Behavioral Research, Therapeutic Approaches*, R. Fox, ed. Springer, New York.

Beckman, L. J. 1975. Women alcoholics: A review of social and psychological studies. *J. Stud. Alcohol, 36*:797–824.

Beckman, L. J. 1976. Alcoholism problems and women: An overview. In *Alcoholism Problems in Women and Children*, M. Greenblatt and M. A. Schuckit, eds. Grune & Stratton, New York.

Beckman, L. J. 1978. Self-esteem of women alcoholics. *J. Stud. Alcohol, 39*: 491–98.

Bell, R. R. 1971. *Social Deviance*. Dorsey Press, Homewood, Ill.

Blane, H. T. 1968. Trends in the prevention of alcoholism. *Psychiatr. Res. Rep., 24*:1–9.

Blane, H. T. and Hill, M. J. 1967. Evaluation of psychotherapy with alcoholics: A critical review. *Q. J. Stud. Alcohol,* 28:76–104.

Bremmer, B. 1967: Alcoholism and fatal accidents. *Q. J. Stud. Alcohol, 28*: 517–28.

Cahalan, D. 1970. *Problem Drinkers.* Jossey-Bass, San Francisco, Calif.

Cahalan, D., Cisin, I., and Crossley, H. 1969. *American Drinking Practices.* Rutgers Center of Alcohol Studies, Monograph No. 6, New Brunswick, N.J.

Cahalan, D. and Room, R. 1974. *Problem Drinking Among American Men.* Rutgers Center of Alcohol Studies, Monograph No. 7, New Brunswick, N.J.

Cahn, S. 1970. *The Treatment of Alcoholics.* Oxford University Press, New York.

Campbell, D. T. and Stanley, J. C. 1963. Experimental and quasi-experimental designs for research on teaching. In *Handbook of Research on Teaching,* N. L. Gage, ed. Rand McNally, Chicago.

Chafetz, M. E., Blane, H. T., and Hill, M. J., eds. 1970. *Frontiers of Alcoholism.* Science House, New York.

Corrigan, E. M. 1974a. *Problem Drinkers Seeking Treatment.* Rutgers Center of Alcohol Studies, Monograph No. 8, New Brunswick, N.J.

Corrigan, E. M. 1974b. Women and problem drinking: Notes on beliefs and facts. *Addict. Dis. Int. J. 1*:215–22.

Cotton, N. S. 1979. The familial incidence of alcoholism: A review. *J. Stud. Alcohol, 40*:89–116.

Cramer, M. J. and Blacker, E. 1966. Social class and drinking experiences of female drunkenness offenders. *J. Health and Human Behav., 7*:276–83.

Curlee, J. 1967. Alcoholic women: some considerations for further research. *Bull. Menninger Clin., 31*:154–63.

Curlee, J. 1968. Women alcoholics. *Fed. Prob., 32*:16–20.

Curlee, J. 1969. Alcoholism and the "empty nest." *Bull. Menninger Clin., 33*:165–71.

Curlee, J. 1970. A comparison of male and female patients at an alcoholism treatment center. *J. Psychol., 74*:239–47.

Curlee, J. 1971. Sex differences in patient attitudes toward alcoholism treatment. *Q. J. Stud. Alcohol, 32*:643–50.

deLint, J. E. 1964. Alcoholism, birth rank and parental deprivation. *Am. J. Psychiatry, 120*:1062–65.

Edwards, G., Hensman, C., and Peto, J. 1972. Drinking troubles among men and women. *Q. J. Stud. Alcohol* (suppl. 6):120–28.

Freed, E. X. 1973. Drug abuse by alcoholics: A review. *Int. J. Addict., 8*: 451–73.

Gerard, D. L. and Sanger, G. 1966. *Out-Patient Treatment of Alcoholism.* Brookside Monograph No. 4, University of Toronto Press, Toronto.

Bibliography

Glatt, M. M. 1961. Treatment results in an English mental hospital alcoholism unit. *Acta. Psychiatr. Scand., 37*:143–68.

Gomberg, E. S. 1974. "Women and alcoholism. In *Women in Therapy,* V. Franks and V. Burtle, eds. Bruner/Mazel, New York.

Gomberg, E. S. 1976. Alcoholism in women. In *The Biology of Alcoholism. Vol. 4: Social Aspects of Alcoholism.* B. Kissin, and H. Begleiter, eds. Plenum Press, New York.

Greenblatt, M. and Schuckit, M. A., eds. 1976. *Alcoholism Problems in Women and Children.* Grune & Stratton, New York.

Haberman, P. W. 1966. Childhood symptoms in children of alcoholics and comparison group parents. *J. Marr. Fam., 28*:152–54.

Haberman, P. W. and Baden, M. 1978. *Alcohol, Other Drugs and Violent Death.* Oxford University Press, New York.

Harper, F. D., ed. 1976. *Alcohol Abuse and Black America.* Douglass, Alexandria, Va.

Heath, D. W. 1975. A critical review of ethnographic studies. In *Research Advances in Alcohol and Drug Problems,* R. J. Gibbins, Y. Israel, H. Kalant, R. E. Popham, W. Schmidt, and R. G. Smart, eds. John Wiley & Sons, New York.

Hollingshead, A. B., 1957. *Two-factor index of social position.* Mimeograph, Yale University, New Haven, Conn.

Horn, J. L. and Wanberg, K. W. 1971. *Females are Different: Some Difficulties in Diagnosing Problems of Alcohol Use in Women.* First Annual Conference, National Institute on Alcohol Abuse and Alcoholism, June 25–26, 1971, Washington, D.C.

Huber, J., ed. 1973. *Changing Women in a Changing Society.* University of Chicago Press, Chicago.

Hunt, M., 1974. *Sexual Behavior in the 1970's.* Playboy Press, Chicago.

Jenkins, S. and Norman, E. 1972. *Filial Deprivation and Foster Care.* Columbia University Press, New York.

Johnson, M. W., DeVries, J. C., and Houghton, M. I. 1966. The female alcoholic. *Nurs. Res., 15*:343–47.

Johnson, P., Armor, D. J., Polich, S., and Stambul, H., 1977. *U.S. Adult Drinking Practices: Time Trends, Social Correlates and Sex Roles.* A working note prepared for the National Institute on Alcohol Abuse and Alcoholism. Rand Corporation, Santa Monica, Calif.

Jones, B. M. and Jones, M. K. 1976a. Male and female intoxication levels for three alcohol doses. *Alcohol Technical Reports.* 5:11–14.

Jones, B. M. and Jones, M. K. 1976b. Women and alcohol: Intoxication, metabolism and the menstrual cycle. In *Alcoholism Problems in Women and Children,* M. Greenblatt and M. A. Schuckit, eds. Grune & Stratton, New York.

Jones, M. C. 1971. Personality antecedents and correlates of drinking patterns in women. *J. Consult. Clin. Psychol., 36*:61–69.

Keller, M. and Efron, V. 1955. Prevalence of alcoholism. *Q. J. Stud. Alcohol, 16*:619–44.

Keller, M. and McCormick, M. 1968. *A Dictionary of Words About Alcohol.* Rutgers Center of Alcohol Studies, New Brunswick, N.J.

Kent, P. 1967. *An American Woman and Alcohol.* Holt, Rinehart & Winston, New York.

Kinsey, A. C., Pomeroy, W. B., and Martin, C. E. 1948. *Sexual Behavior in the Human Male.* W. B. Saunders, Philadelphia.

Kinsey, B. A. 1966. *The Female Alcoholic.* Charles C Thomas, Springfield, Ill.

Knupfer, G. 1963. *California Drinking Practices Study.* State of California, Department of Public Health, Report No. 6 (April), Berkeley, Calif.

Langner, T. S. 1962. A twenty-two item screening score for psychiatric symptoms indicating impairment. *J. Health Human Behav., 3*:269–276.

Levine, J. 1955. The sexual adjustment of alcoholics: A clinical study of a selected sample. *Q. J. Stud. Alcohol, 16*:675–80.

Lindbeck, V. L. 1972. The woman alcoholic: A review of the literature. *Int. J. Addict., 7*:567–80.

Lisansky, E. S. 1957. Alcoholism in women: Social and psychological concomitants. *Q. J. Stud. Alcohol, 18*:588–623.

Lisansky, E. S. 1958. The woman alcoholic. *Understanding Alcoholism: The Annals of the American Academy of Political and Social Science, 315*: 73–81 (January).

Lolli, G. 1953. Alcoholism in women. *Conn. Rev. Alcoholism, 5*:9–11.

McCord, W. and McCord, J. 1960. *Origins of Alcoholism.* Stanford University Press, Stanford, Calif.

Madden, J. S. and Jones, D. 1972. Bout and continuous drinking in alcoholism. *Brit. J. Addict., 67*:245–50.

Martin, J. 1977. The fetal alcohol syndrome. In *Alcohol, Health and Research World, 1*:8–12.

Miller, D. and Jang M. 1977. Children of alcoholics: A twenty year longitudinal study. *Soc. Work Res. Abstr., 13*:4 (Winter).

Mulford, H. A. 1977. Women and men problem drinking: Sex differences in patients served by Iowa's Community Alcoholism Centers. *J. Stud. Alcohol, 38*:1627–39.

Mulford, H. A. and Miller, D. E. 1960. Drinking in Iowa. IV. Preoccupation with alcohol and definitions of alcohol, heavy drinking and trouble due to drinking. *Q. J. Stud. Alcohol, 21*:279–91.

Murphree, H. B. 1976. Some possible origins of alcoholism. In *Alcohol and Alcohol Problems.* W. J. Filstead, J. J. Rossi, and M. Keller, eds. M. Ballinger, Cambridge, Mass.

Myerson, D. J. 1959. Clinical observations on a group of alcoholic prisoners, with special reference to women. *Q. J. Stud. Alcohol, 20*:555–72.

National Foundation, March of Dimes. 1977. *Facts.* White Plains, N.Y.

Nie, N. H., Hull, C. H., Jenkins, J. G., Steinbrenner, K., and Bent, D. H. 1975. *Statistical Package for the Social Sciences.* McGraw-Hill, New York.

Parry, H. J. 1971. Patterns of psychotropic drug use among American adults. *J. Drug Issues, 1*:269–73.

Pemberton, D. A. 1967. A comparison of the outcome of treatment in female and male alcoholism. *Br. J. Psychiatry, 113*:367–73.

Pollack, M. and Gittelman, R. L. 1964. The siblings of childhood schizophrenics. *Am. J. Orthopsychiatry, 34*:868–73.

Rathod, N. H. and Thompson, I. G. 1971. Women alcoholics: A clinical study. *Q. J. Stud. Alcohol, 32*:45–52.

Ray, O. S. 1978. *Drugs, Society and Human Behavior.* C. V. Mosby, St. Louis.

Rickels, K., ed. 1968. *Non-specific Factors in Drug Therapy.* Charles C Thomas, Springfield, Ill.

Rimmer, J., Pitts, F. N., Reich, T., and Winokur, G. 1971. Alcoholism. II. Sex, socioeconomic status and race in two hospitalized samples. *Q. J. Stud. Alcohol, 32*:942–52.

Rimmer, J., Reich, T., and Winokur, G. 1972. Alcoholism. V. Diagnosis and clinical variation among alcoholics. *Q. J. Stud. Alcohol, 33*:658–66.

Room, R. 1968. *Amount of Drinking and Alcoholism.* Mimeographed paper prepared for presentation at the 28th International Congress on Alcohol and Alcoholism, September 15–20, 1968, Washington, D.C.

Schuckit, M. A. and Morrissey, E. R. 1976. Alcoholism in women: Some clinical and social perspectives with an emphasis on possible subtypes. In *Alcoholism Problems in Women and Children,* M. Greenblatt and M. A. Schuckit, eds. Grune & Stratton, New York.

Schuckit, M. A., Pitts, F. N., Reich, T., King, L. J., and Winokur, G. 1969. Alcoholism. I. Two types of alcoholism in women. *Arch. Gen. Psychiatry, 20*:301–6.

Sclare, A. B. 1970. The female alcoholic; A clinical study. *Br. J. Addict., 65*:99–107.

Sherfey, M. J. 1955. Psychopathy and character structure in chronic alcoholism. In *Etiology of Chronic Alcoholism,* O. Diethelm, ed. Charles C Thomas, Springfield, Ill.

Siegel, S. 1956. *Non-parametric Statistics for the Behavioral Sciences.* McGraw-Hill, New York.

Streissguth, A. P. 1976. Maternal alcoholism and the outcome of pregnancy: A review of the fetal alcohol syndrome. In *Alcoholism Problems in Women and Children,* M. Greenblatt and M. A. Schuckit, eds. Grune & Stratton, New York.

United States Bureau of the Census, 1976. Number, timing and duration of marriages and divorces in the United States: June 1975. *Current Population Reports,* Series P-20 No. 297. United States Government Printing Office, Washington, D.C.

United States Department of Health, Education and Welfare, 1968. *Patients in Mental Institutions.* Part A, Table 3, p. 59, United States Government Printing Office, Washington, D.C.

United States Department of Health, Education and Welfare, 1969. In-patient admissions to state and county mental hospitals. *Public Health Service Publication,* Statistical Note 49, Table 4, p. 133.

United States Department of Health, Education and Welfare, 1971. In-patient admission to state and county mental hospitals. *Public Health Service Publication.* Statistical Note 49, Table H:11–13 (April).

United States Department of Health, Education and Welfare: National Institute on Alcohol Abuse and Alcoholism, 1974. *Alcohol and Health.* Second report to the United States Congress from The Secretary of Health, Education and Welfare.

Wall, J. H. 1937. A study of alcoholism in women. *Am. J. Psychiatry, 93*: 943–53.

Wanberg, K. W. and Horn, J. L. 1970. Alcoholism symptom patterns of men and women: A comparative study. *Q. J. Stud. Alcohol, 31*:40–61.

Wanberg, K. W. and Knapp, J. 1970. Differences in drinking symptoms and behavior of men and women alcoholics. *Br. J. Addict., 64*:347–55.

Warner, R. H. and Rosett, H. L. 1975. The effects of drinking on offspring: An historical survey of the American and British literature. *J. Stud. Alcohol, 36*:1395–1420.

Wilkinson, P., Santamaria, J. N., Rankin, J. G., and Martin, D. 1969. Epidemiology of alcoholism: Social data and drinking patterns of a sample of Australian alcoholics. *Med. J. Aust., 1*:1020–25.

Wilsnack, S. 1973. Sex-role identity in female alcoholism. *J. Abnorm. Psychol., 82*:253–61.

Winokur, G. and Clayton, P. J. 1968. Family history studies. IV. Comparison of male and female alcoholics. *Q. J. Stud. Alcohol, 29*:885–91.

Winokur, G., Reich, T., Rimmer, J., and Pitts, F. N. 1970. Alcoholism. III. Diagnosis and familiar psychiatric illness in 259 alcoholic husbands. *Arch. Gen. Psychiatry, 23*:104–11.

Wood, H. P. and Duffy, E. L. 1966. Psychological factors in alcoholic women. *Am. J. Psychiatry, 123*:341–45.

Index

Abortion, 37
Abstainer
 background variables, 152
 rare drinkers, 140, 151
 regression analysis, 140
Age, 18, 20, 22, 23
Agency
 data, 137
 entry, 19–20, 24
 selection, 13
Alcohol consumption, 38–43
 average amount, 42
Alcoholics Anonymous, 11–12, 24, 147–53
 emotional health, 149
Alcoholism
 as dependency, 65
 family, 108–11
Amark, 111
Amphetamines, 51
Analysis plan, 15–26
Anderson, 127–30, 163, 170
Armor, 91, 105, 132, 139, 154

Baden, 61
Bailey, 76
Barbiturates, 51–52

Bar drinking, 44–45, 63
Beckman, 4, 110
Beer, 44
Beverage, alcohol, 44. *See also specific beverage*
Binge drinkers, 40, 43
Birth defects, 92–93
Blacker, 45, 58
Black women, 18, 20, 50, 160. *See also* Race
 social drinking, 160
 treatment outcome, 140–44
Bremmer, 51

Cahalan, 6, 19, 38, 42, 64, 72, 90, 121, 152, 159
Cahn, 6
Cambridge-Somerville, 125
Catholic, 18, 20, 23–24, 64
Chafetz, 4
Children, 4, 92–97, 102–3
 attention by mother, 103
 birth defects, 92–93
 effects, 95–97
 negligence, 94
 separations, 94

Cirrhosis, 6
Cisin, 19, 38, 42, 64, 90, 121, 152, 159
Clayton, 108, 111
Cocaine, 53
Cognitive functioning, 68
Controlled drinking, 146
Corrigan, 6, 8, 72, 166
Courts, 94
Co-workers, 47
Cramer, 45, 58
Crossley, 19, 38, 42, 64, 90, 121, 152, 159
Curlee, 4–5, 7, 51
Curran, 8

Daily drinkers, 40
Data coding, 14, 175
Demographic variables. *See* Independent variables
Dependency
  physiological, 54, 65
  psychological, 54
Dependent variables, 19
Depressants, 53
Depression, 7, 37
Divorced women, 18, 20. *See also* Marriage
Drinking, 42, 48, 50. *See also* Alcohol consumption; Follow-up
  alone, 3, 46, 47
  in bars, 44–45, 47
  categories, 19, 20, 41
  with co-workers, 47
  effects, 163–65
  emotional health and treatment, 147–51
  frequency, 40
  highs, 65
  at home, 44
  maintenance, 54
  measurement, 59
  morning, 65
  norms, 124
  onset, 7, 33, 157–61
  parental attitudes, 109
  quantity, 40–43, 83
  secrecy in, 8, 48–50
  siblings, 111–12
  specific life situations, 3, 37
  troubles, 8
Drugs, 51–54, 120, 160. *See also* individual drugs
Duffy, 8, 47

Education, 16–17
Edwards, 8, 19, 72

Effects of drinking, 163–65
Efron, 6
Emotional health status, 19, 62, 75–78, 119
  initial and follow-up, 141–43, 147–51
  regression analysis, 143
Employment, 62
  employers, 8
  follow-up, 144
  status, 16
  unemployed, 45
Entry treatment agency, 12, 19–20, 23–24
Escapist drinking. *See* Social-escapist index
Etiology, 112, 114, 161–63

Family members, 47, 108–11
  abstinence, parental, 109–10
  early relationships, 115
  interference, 79
  parental problem drinking, 109–11
  relatives, alcoholism rates among, 108
Father, 108–9
Fetal alcohol syndrome, 92–93
Fink, 177
First drink, 33
Follow-up of treatment
  abstainers and rare-occasion drinkers, 140, 151
  alcohol consumption, change in, 138–39
  background variables, 139–40
  emotional health, 141–44, 147–51
  employment, 144
  interviewed vs. not interviewed, 172, 174–75
  interviews, 173
  treatment combinations, 147–51
Franck drawing, 169
Freed, 51
Frequency of drinking, 40
Friends, 44, 48, 115
  changed, 67
  close, 159
Frigidity, 8. *See also* Sexual behavior
F value, 178

Gerard, 6, 13, 132
Gittelman, 113
Glazier, 130*n*
Greenblatt, 75
Grundy, 177

Index

Haberman, 61, 93
Hallucinogens, 53
Hard liquor, 44
Harper, 160
Health, 8, 79–80, 115. *See also* Emotional health status
Heroin, 120
Hidden drinking, 8, 49
Homeless women, 11
Horn, 4, 47
Hospitals, 6, 11
Housewife, 9, 16, 20, 23, 159
Hunt, 102
Husband, 4–5, 11, 14, 97–103, 158
 interviews, 97–103

Illnesses or accidents, 37
Income, 16–17
 source, 17
Independent variables, 15–29
 relationship to others, 24–29
Index, 187
Inpatient, 24
Interference, drinking, 78–83
 background variables, 81–83
 correlations, 80–81
 in family, social, job, and health areas, 78–80
 self-rating, 79
Interviews, 11, 170
 interviewers, 170–71
 interviewing loss, 113
 procedures, 171
Interview schedules, 169
 agency questionnaires, 170
 husband, 170
 sister, non-alcoholic, 170
 women, 169
Isolation index, 68. *See also* Social life

Jang, 105
Jewish, 18
Jobs, 8
 functioning, 79
 loss, 37
 satisfaction, 115
Johnson, 23, 47, 62, 166
Jones, 6, 124, 128

Keller, 6, 59, 133
Kinsey, 101
Knapp, 47
Knupfer, 51

Langer, 76, 141
Lesbian, 70
Levine, 7
Li, 177
Life situations, 7, 158, 163
Lisansky, 4–5, 50, 58, 109, 110–12
Locale, 15, 20, 25
Lolli, 7
Loneliness, 38
Longitudinal study, 11, 105

Ma, 106
Maintenance dosage, 146
Male-female ratio, 6
Marijuana, 52, 120
Marriage, 5, 18, 20, 87–90
 census data, 105n
 marital status, 14, 16, 18, 20, 22, 27
 outside employment status, 20, 25
 problems, 37
McCord and McCord, 125
McCormick, 59, 133
McNemar test, 179
Mean defined, 178
Menopause, 37
Mental health, sisters, 115
Methadone, 120
Miller, 105
Morning drinking, 65
Morrissey, 58
Mother, 4, 91–92, 93–97
Moving. *See specific life situation*
Mulford, 46, 53, 72, 74, 108, 110–12
Multiple regression, 179
Murphree, 54
Myerson, 8

National Foundation/March of Dimes, 106
Neighbors, 47–48
Never married, 18, 20
Non-alcoholic sisters. *See* Sisters
Normal drinking, 146
Nurses. *See* Professional

Opiates, 53
Outpatient, 24

Parry, 53
Physiological dependency, 54, 65
Polich, 91, 105, 132, 139, 154

Police, 8. *See also* Troubles
Pollack, 113
Poverty, 17–18
Pregnancy, 92
Pressures for drinking, 36
Private physicians, 6
Problem drinkers, 5, 7, 110
Professional women, 13, 15–16, 20, 28, 42, 48
Prognosis, 3, 9
Promiscuity, 8. *See also* Sexual behavior
Protestant, 18, 20, 23–24, 64
Psychiatric disorder, 76
Psychological dependency, 54
Psychoneurosis, 76
Psychotropic drugs, 53

Quantity-Frequency-Variability index, 59n. *See also* Alcohol consumption; Drinking

Race, 18, 20, 27
Rare-occasion drinkers, 140, 151
Rathod, 51
Ratio, 5–6
Ray, 159
Refusals, interview, 113
Regression analysis
  abstainers, 150
  abstainers and dependent variables, 151
  abstainers and rare-occasion drinkers, 151
  emotional health score, 143
Rejection, social, of drinking women, 66, 123
Relatives. *See* Family members
Reliability data, 42
Religion, 18, 20, 23–24
  organized, 65
  taboos, 158
Restaurant drinking, 44–45
Rickels, 125
Role confusion, 125–27
  indicators, 127
  parental expectations, 126
Room, 39, 74
Rosset, 53

Sampling, 12–13
Sanger, 6, 13, 132
Scales, 19
School, 115
Schuckit, 58, 75, 111
Sedatives, 51–52
Separated women. *See* Marriage
Sex role, 127–28, 163
Sexual behavior, 7, 68–71
  orientation, 70
  response, 62
  satisfaction, 70
Sherfey, 109
Siblings, 112–13
Siegel, 177
Sign test, 114, 178
Single women. *See* Marriage
Sisters, 112–30
  as mothers, 124
  children of, 124
  drinking reasons, 121
  emotional health, 119
  interviews, 14
  life situation comparisons, 115
  matched pairs, 117–30
  role confusion, 125–27
  sex roles, 127–28
Sleeping pills, 52, 120, 160
Social agencies, 6, 94
Social drinking. *See* Social-escapist index
Social-escapist index, 19, 50–51, 120–22
Social life, 67–68
  isolation index, 68
Socioeconomic status, 16–17, 19–20, 26–27, 140–41, 150–51
SPSS, 177
Stambul, 91, 105, 132, 139, 154
Standard deviation, 178
State and county mental hospitals, 6
State-supported alcoholism clinics, 6
Statistical analysis, 21
  procedures, 177–79
  significance, 177–78
Stigma, 62–63
  shame, 3
Stimulants, 52–53
Student-Newman-Keuls range test, 179
Suburban women, 12–15, 20, 42, 134–35
Surveys, national, 159

t test, 178
Teachers. *See* Professional women
Telephone, 47
Telescoped drinking, 34–36

Theory. *See* Family members; Role confusion; Sex role
Thompson, 51
Tolerance, 54
Tranquilizers, 52, 54, 120, 160
 minor, 51
Treatment, 9, 131–54
 combinations, 148
 outcome, race, 152
 outcome, socioeconomic, 152
 prior treatment, 145
Tremors, 54
Troubles, 8, 19, 62, 72–75
Twenty-Two Item Screening Score. *See* Emotional health status

Ultrafemininity. *See* Sex role
Urban women, 12–15, 20, 42, 135–36
Validity, 42

Variables. *See* Dependent variables; Independent variables

Wall, 7
Wanberg, 4, 47
Warner, 92
White women, 18, 20, 50, 160. *See also* Race
Widow. *See* Marriage
Wife, 5, 91–92
Wilcoxin matched-pairs signed-ranks test, 179
Wilsnack, 4, 127, 170
Wine, 44
Winokur, 108, 111
Withdrawal, 65
Women drink less, 8
 in treatment, 12
Wood, 8, 47, 108